P9-AQB-813

. . . Public
. . . Relations
. . . for School
. . . Library
. . . Media
. . . Programs

500 WAYS TO INFLUENCE PEOPLE AND WIN FRIENDS
FOR YOUR SCHOOL LIBRARY MEDIA CENTER

Helen F. Flowers

WITHDRAWN

MONTGOMERY COUNTY PUBLIC SCHOOLS
PROFESSIONAL LIBRARY
850 HUNGERFORD DRIVE
ROCKVILLE, MARYLAND 20850

1116714
6-98

Neal-Schuman Publishers, Inc.
New York   London

Published by Neal-Schuman Publishers, Inc.
100 Varick Street
New York, NY 10013

Copyright © 1998 by Helen F. Flowers

All rights reserved. Reproduction of this book, in whole or in part, without written permission of the publisher is prohibited.

Printed and bound in the United States of America.

Library of Congress Cataloging-in-Publication Data

Flowers, Helen F.
    Public relations for school library media programs : 500 ways to influence people and win friends for your school library media center / Helen F. Flowers.
        p.   cm.
    Includes bibliographical references and index.
    ISBN 1–55570–320–8
    1. Public relations—School libraries—United States.
2. Public relations—Instructional materials centers—United States. I. Title
Z675.S3F55 1998
C21.7—dc21   98–11470
                                                CIP

With gratitude and affection this book is dedicated to four educators who had a profound influence on my life:

W. E. Burton
Frances Henne
Alma Hill
Anne Parrish Markham

CONTENTS

FIGURES

ACKNOWLEDGMENTS

Thanks to Eileen Mulcahy, my colleague and friend for twenty-five years, with whom many of the ideas presented here were developed. No two people ever worked more harmoniously together, accomplished more for students, and had as much fun doing it as we did.

Thanks also to the many library media staff members over the years who contributed to creating an atmosphere in the library that made for good public relations or who played a part in carrying out public relations projects. How fortunate I was to work with Bonnie Cestra, Eleanor Koltz, Pat Veraldo, Barbara Mauro, Connie De Louise, Eileen Mayott, Theresa Garguilo, Maria Sparacio, Star Paige, Wayna Beaudrie, and Ellen Ballin.

Thanks to the contributors who shared their ideas with me, and to those media specialists with whom, over the years, I enjoyed conversations late into the night about library media matters. Media specialists who answered my calls for ideas with their own successful PR techniques include:

Beatrice E. Angus, Director
Madison-Oneida Area School
    Library System
Sherrill, New York

Susan D. Ballard, Director
Library Media Services
Londonderry School District
Londonderry, New Hampshire

Ellen Ballin
Islip Terrace Junior High School
Islip Terrace, New York

Catherine M. Beyers
Southern Bluffs Elementary School
La Crosse, Wisconsin

Sandra Block
Instructional Supervisor
Dade Country Public Schools
Library Media Services
Miami, Florida

Deborah Coleman
Barnwell Elementary School
Barnwell, South Carolina

Carolyn Giambra
North High School
Williamsville, New York

Judy Gray
Nottingham High School
Syracuse, New York

Susan McCormick
Sachem High School North
Lake Ronkonkoma, New York

Roy D. Miller (retired)
Brooklyn Public Library
Brooklyn, New York

June Muldner
George H. Nichols School
Endicott, New York

Laura Saraceno
Jennie F. Snapp Middle School
Endicott, New York

Joel Shoemaker
South East Junior High School
Iowa City, Iowa

Harriet S. Selverstone
Norwalk High School
Norwalk, Connecticut

Rocco A. Staino
North Salem Schools
North Salem, New York

Thanks to Virginia Mathews, who has inspired us all with her passion and persistence in the cause of exemplary library services to children. This book was her idea, and her guidance as I wrote it was invaluable.

And thanks also to Conner Flowers, best friend and husband, honor graduate of the Flying Fingers School of Keyboarding, for his total support.

PREFACE

I have chosen to write this book in an informal, conversational style rather than as a formal, academic treatise. My purpose is to speak directly to you, elementary and secondary library media specialists, and to present to you practical ideas for communicating a vision of quality library media programs. You will need to communicate this vision to decision makers, to the community, and to media center users as you work to gain their support and promote the use of library media services. The public relations techniques included here, however, are by no means limited to school library media specialists but may also be useful to those in other library settings.

You will read some of the strategies listed in each chapter and comment to yourself, "I've been doing that for years!" But bear in mind that the same information may be considered novel and challenging by someone else. Just remember that even the expert can learn new strategies for doing a little differently and more effectively what has already been done before.

You may ask yourself how you can possibly do everything included here, given the constraints on your time. Never fear, nobody has that much time, but over several years you may be able to try many of these "tricks." The point is, pick and choose the ones you need and the ones you are able to do, but *do something*.

Public Relations for School Library Media Programs: 500 Ways to Influence People and Win Friends for Your School Library Media Center is arranged by the groups of recipients your public relations (PR) efforts will target. Among your targets are, of course, students, faculty, and building administrators; but you ought not to forget that beyond the walls of the building in which you work are other groups that are potential supporters and users of library media services. These groups include district administrators, board of education members, parents and others in the community, and elected officials at all levels. Each chapter includes a discussion of why that group should get your attention, as well as a list of ways to promote the use of services and to gain support. Recommendations for preparing reports and printed materials are also included.

SOME EXPLANATIONS

Much of the material included in the book comes from my own long experience in a public senior high school located in a supportive school district with a board of education that employed a surprisingly large number of enlightened administrators.

I would wish as much for every library media specialist. Some of the suggestions are those used by media specialist friends over the years and are not attributable to any particular person. I thank them, whoever they are. Others were contributed especially for this book by generous media specialists who responded to my call for ideas.

I have included some samples of items mentioned in the text—a PR plan, flyers to teachers, forms, announcements, invitations, bookmark and display ideas, reports, and the like. With one exception, I used all of these printed pieces in my school—plus many more that have not survived retirement and a long-distance move. Eileen Mulcahy, with whom I worked for many years, and I developed together or separately the ideas for these pieces, some of which I have somewhat reworked for this book. Although they were used in a high school situation, they should be adaptable to any level. I hope that you will gather ideas from them. You are free to adapt and use these as you see fit without seeking permission.

School districts and their organizations vary considerably. When examples of school district policy and structure are discussed here, don't be concerned if they sound nothing like yours; insert your own where applicable. Goals and results are usually similar.

Communities vary, too. Knowing the attitudes of the people in your community is important in determining the success of your public relations program. Would a display of ghost stories for Halloween be offensive to a significant segment of your students' parents? A public relations thrust in a high school may be inappropriate in an elementary school setting. When designing your PR efforts and selecting strategies from those offered in this book, use common sense. Ask yourself "What will fit my school and my community?" After all, your purpose is to win friends for your library, not to create controversy.

To avoid having to write "he/she" when a singular pronoun is needed, I have chosen to alternate, more or less, between using "he" and "she." Please do not read any gender bias into the use of these pronouns, for none is intended.

I've been around long enough to prefer the word "library" for where we work, and "librarian" for what we are. However, "library media specialist" and "library media center" convey more fully what we do and the place in which we do it than do the older terms. In this book, I use various titles but imply no distinction among them.

I have used the word "publication" to mean any communication printed (produced) by any method. In my mind, it refers to preparation and photocopying that is done in your own media center or in your own building, as well as more professional processes.

Media specialists who contributed ideas are listed with their schools in the Acknowledgments. Materials I used from published and copyrighted sources are cited in the text by author, and are listed at the end of the book in the References. I have also provided a selection of titles for further reading that you may want to examine. Some of them make no direct references to libraries but deal with topics we should all be more familiar with as we strive to persuade, influence, lead, and communicate with potential library supporters.

INTRODUCTION

PUBLIC RELATIONS: ESSENTIAL TO EVERYTHING YOU DO

The school library media program does not exist in a vacuum. It is an integral part of what goes on in every area of the school. The media center is one of the few departments in the school with responsibility to every student, every teacher, and every other department. Research shows that students with access to well-supported school library media programs attain higher levels of academic achievement than do students without such access (Lance 1992). A quality library media program must have a qualified staff and adequate funding if it is to be an indispensable part of the education the school offers.

School library media specialists know these things, and while there are administrators and other decision makers in some school districts who recognize these truths, by no means do they all—or even a majority. Similarly, not all members of the teaching staff are fully aware of what the services of the media center can do for them and their students. Do not assume, however, that every school staff or every community wants a quality library media program, as hard as that is to believe: They are not likely to miss what they have never had. We cannot just wait around for them to realize eventually that a quality library program is essential to a quality school. It is our job to create the desire. We must let administrators, teachers, parents, and the community in general know how an excellent library program contributes to the academic success of students and helps teachers to be better teachers. And when teachers and students are successful, administrators' success ratings improve. The public relations program you put in place may need to start with such a basic idea as creating the desire for an outstanding library media program.

You, the library media specialist, are the most important element in devising an effective public relations effort for your media center. You are the designer, the developer, and the implementor of these plans and activities. This is not to say that you do not utilize the time and talents of other people, but the burden is yours—as is the pleasure that comes from success. A successful public relations plan cannot be laid on from an administrator's office. It must come from you.

You create the atmosphere that makes the library media center either a warm and welcoming place or one that is cold and forbidding. Your attitudes about your mission and that of the library media center in the school affect not only how successful you are in promoting your program, but also how you are perceived by students, teachers, and administrators.

LET DECISION MAKERS KNOW

A good school library media program fosters high-level literacy and thinking skills, information literacy, and inquiry. One of the jobs of the media specialist is to ensure that decision makers know the full scope and purpose of the media center and support it, and that teachers and students are aware of the media center services and utilize them. The school district's board of education—the body that funds and sets the policies of the entire district educational operation—must be included, along with parents and other community members, on the list of those who should be made more knowledgeable about the part the media center plays in the academic success of students. Not the least among those who must be made aware of the importance of libraries in the lives of students are legislators at both the state and national levels.

Library media centers need the understanding and support of all these groups in order to succeed, and public relations is the vital means for ensuring that success. Every library media specialist has the responsibility to know these decision makers at all levels and to communicate to them continually and with passion and persistence the need youngsters have for libraries.

Each of us should have a carefully honed, well-developed vision of what the school library media program should and can be. We must know precisely what we believe about library media service to youngsters, and why we believe it. Our jobs require a fierce commitment to sharing, communicating, and articulating our vision to others. We need to help decision makers join with us in this vision. Our efforts must be ongoing and persistent—not for our own benefit, but for the students with whom we work. Failure to do this puts library media programs in peril.

WHAT IS PR?

I consider library media center public relations as:

- our efforts to gain and maintain support for library media center programs, and

- our efforts to promote and encourage the use of library media center services.

We must balance these two aspects of our PR efforts. To provide the broad range of services that make up the library media program, we need an adequate budget. At the same time we are reminding decision makers to fund our programs, we must also be at work informing faculty and students of the services we have available to them and trying to expand the scope of our services—as well as increasing the number of users until we reach everyone in the school community. We are constantly seeking funding to maintain the level of services we offer, and at the same time trying to offer more services—thereby making it necessary to seek more funding. This makes for an exciting and challenging juggling act. Nobody ever promised us it would be easy.

By keeping administrators aware of the role the media center plays in the instructional mission of the school, we contribute to the justification for maintaining and increasing support for staff, materials, equipment, and space. Everyone in the school community and the wider community must come to understand that the media center's resources make possible individualized learning for each student as well as teaching for each teacher. The library media center need not be confined to books and data in other formats held within its own physical space, but also is the entryway to regional, national, even international, resources for students.

The purpose of this book is to offer ideas for communicating our library media vision to decision makers, to the community, and to those who use our services. To a large extent, public relations depends on communications, and communication implies an exchange of thoughts, ideas, opinions. Too often our efforts are spent on sending messages, with little attention given to receiving messages in return. It is to our advantage to know what our publics think about library media services. Search for ways to make it easy for users and your community to communicate with you. How do students and teachers rate the services they receive? What do administrators see as our role? What additional services do our users want from the library media center? What is the community's opinion of the library media program? Feedback provides us with information indicating public expectations and information we can then use in planning for change. By asking questions and listening for answers, we evaluate our product and performance and identify areas to focus on in future public relations efforts.

POLLING AND SURVEYS

Polling our students, faculty, and administrators is an excellent way to gather information about attitudes toward our services. If the task seems formidable, consider joining forces with other media specialists in the district to survey all schools. Designing a questionnaire that can be used districtwide will be less difficult if it is a shared responsibility.

If the district central administration plans to survey the community, be sure questions about library media services are included, and offer to help construct the questions. School libraries are an all-but-invisible component of the instructional program, sometimes because they are taken for granted, but often because they are overlooked by those who are not kept aware of their essential role for all students.

The popularity of political polls and the use to which the resulting information is put does not escape us as we see political campaigns heat up. The Gallup/Phi Delta Kappa Educational Poll annually surveys a sample of some 2,000 adults from across the country to learn the public's attitudes toward the public schools. Each year results provide many school districts with indications of the direction they should take and issues the public expects them to address. Questions about library media services have not been included in the questionnaires in recent years, although feedback from a national survey would be useful in planning library media policy. We should urge our leaders in the American Library Association (ALA) to press for the inclusion of library media services in this influential national poll.

The ideas offered here to promote support for and the use of library media programs have been used successfully by many library media specialists. Some ideas may be useful to you in their entirety, others may contain a useful element, some may spark a different idea of your own. Take for your own purposes whatever you find here, and ask yourself what would work for you. Few of us have the time to start from scratch, so we must think in terms of adapting, rewording, reshaping what others have done.

TIME TO DO PR

Time is a consideration that cannot be denied, so how can we possibly find time to carry out public relations projects when every minute of every day is already overscheduled? The answer is to examine our priorities. In rethinking what has to be done, we may have to jettison some jobs, shift responsibility for them to someone else, or devise new ways of doing them.

One library media specialist said, "I don't have time to write and send reports to my principal. Anyway, she already knows what a great job I'm doing with the students." Don't count on it! As Hartzell writes, "We are all attracted to the notion that something of quality will enjoy support just because it is so obviously right," but "research and experience show that this is a . . . fundamentally flawed idea" (Hartzell 1994, p. 28). Being good at your job is not enough. Principals need "talking points," fresh examples, phrases that they can use to support your efforts.

This may sound like some of those stories from *McGuffey's Reader* that teach a great moral lesson, but that same library media specialist was "excessed" when the school district downsized staff, and now she has time in abundance. Her former students have access to fewer library media services, and they see a library media specialist only one day a week. Someone has said that a library without a librarian is just a room with books. By the same token, without a library media specialist, a library media center has no library media program. Obviously, and in hindsight, that media specialist should have found time to specify to her principal the value to students of the media program and the importance of the library media specialist in planning and implementing the program. And to do so in writing.

Having a public relations plan in place may not in and of itself prevent the reduction in funding for media services, staffing, and materials. In fact, an excellent public relations program will do nothing for an inadequate library media program. However, school districts in hard financial times are more likely to preserve those educational programs that have proven their effectiveness—especially if a lot of people know about them. Every library media specialist, then, has the professional obligation to communicate to decision makers how intrinsic to student achievement are the media center and the media specialist—it is extremely unlikely that anyone else will do it for us. We hope that this book will help you develop and implement a public relations plan for your library media center.

YOUR PUBLIC RELATIONS PLAN

Of the activities we perform among our daily chores, many can be classified as "public relations." We display new materials; mount bulletin boards and display cases; talk with teachers, administrators, and students; and do a host of other things. These activities can expand the audience for our services and keep administrators up-to-date on what we are doing. But support for and use of our services in the education of our youngsters are so important that they cannot be left to chance. Wishing won't do the job. What you must have is a structured plan of action, a public relations plan.

We can look at developing a public relations plan in somewhat the same way we plan for an automobile trip. We ask ourselves the same questions:

- *Where are we now?* What is the current situation that makes us want to be somewhere else? What is our starting point? For example, do last year's statistics reveal what you suspected, that kids are not reading? If so, not only are those kids missing out on fiction and other imaginative literature but also on developing the pleasure in habitual reading that marks truly literate people. Have you noticed that you are involved with fewer than half the teachers in your building in the development of their lesson plans and instructional units?

- *Where do we want to go?* Do we want to change the status quo in some way? What is it we want to achieve? What is our destination: more reading, more discussion of the meaning of what is read, greater involvement in teacher planning?

- *How are we going to get there?* What activities will help us reach our destination? What routes will we take: booktalks, more attractive displays, reading contests? How about speaking at department meetings, sending flyers to the faculty, one-to-one conversations with individual teachers, developing a relationship with parents and civic groups?

- *How will we know when we have arrived at our destination?* At the end of the trip, do figures show that reading has increased? Are teachers coming to us more often and incorporating more media center activities in their unit plans? Are they more receptive to us and more willing to share in planning with us?

Other questions to ask ourselves in the planning phase are:

- *How long is the trip going to take?* What is the time frame for our plan? What are some interim objectives along the way?

- *When do we plan to get to certain benchmarks along the way?* When will certain activities be accomplished?

- *Who is going to help with the driving?* Are there aides, volunteers (both student and adult), or others we can count on to help us reach our destination?

The public relations plan, then, is made up of:

- A statement of our starting point (where we are now)

- The goal we want to achieve, supported by objectives along the way (where we are going)

- The activities we will undertake to reach our goal (how do we get there)

- The time frame in which the activities will be accomplished (how long is the trip)

- Who will do the activities (who helps drive)

- The dates the activities will be completed (reaching certain points)

- Evaluating what has been accomplished (did we get where we were going)

Some people decide to do a few public relations activities, perhaps jotting down some sketchy notes and carrying the rest of them in their heads. This is like setting out on a trip without knowing where you are going or the route you will take. We know only too well how likely it is you will forget your purpose and let your public relations efforts be overrun by daily pressures.

Public relations is a long-term benefit; its rewards appear only over time. So write out your plan and post it where you can see it. Discuss your plan with your administrator and leave a copy with her. It is more difficult to overlook and forget about the plan if it is in full view, and if others know about it. Figure Intro-1 contains a sample PR plan you can use as a guideline in setting up your own.

Begin your plan with a short statement about what you want to change and the time period your plan will cover. You may want to focus your plan on one group (students, teachers, administrators, community, or state or national legislators) or on several. For example, this year you may want to concentrate your heavy guns on your building administrators while continuing to send flyers to teachers and writing articles for the school newspaper. Whatever you choose to do, put it in writing.

Goal setting is deciding what you want to achieve. Most of us touched on this topic in education courses and were left with the feeling of frustration, a vague memory

Figure Intro–1 Sample PR Plan

Current Situation: 587 hard cover volumes (avg. cost $25, total cost of $14,675) disappeared from the HS LMC in 1995–96 school yr.

Beech South High School Library Media Center Planning Matrix

Goal: Reduce theft of LMC materials by 80% by persuading Board of Education to fund purchase of a security system for the LMC in time for inclusion in the 1997–98 school district budget.

Objectives	Activities	Timeline	Person(s) Responsible	Date Completed
A. Get principal's support	A.1. Prepare Loss Report incl. statistics for last 3 yrs.	June 30, 1996	Libn. help from Lib. secretary and aides	
	A.2. Meet with prin. to discuss impact of problem on students.	July 15, 1996	Libn.	
	A.3. Ask prin. to join me in a visit to Maple Hill H.S. to observe their security sys.	Sept. 20, 1996	Libn., prin.	
	A.4. Get proposals from vendors.	Oct. 15, 1996	Sec'y schedule visits.	
	A.5. Prepare purchase proposal.	Nov. 1, 1996	Libn./Maple Hill libn.	
	A.6. Discuss purchase plan with prin.	Nov. 5, 1996	Libn.	
	A.7. Ask prin. to discuss problem and plan with District Curriculum Coordinator.			
B. Get dept. chairs' support	B.1. Meet with chairs whose depts. are most heavily affected.	Nov. 10, 1996	Libn.	
	B.2. Share Loss Report with them and ask them to support purchase proposal by sending report on impact of lost materials on their students to Curr. Coord.	Nov. 28, 1996	Libn. Eng., For. Lang., Health, Soc. Stud. Dept. chairs	
C. Get support of District Curriculum Coordinator	C.1. Present Loss Report and Discuss impact on student resource-based projects.	Dec. 1, 1996	Libn.—Use Dept. Chair Statements	
	C.2. Discuss cost of lost materials, cost of replacement, and cost of security sys.	Dec. 1, 1996	Libn.	
D. Get Supt.'s support.	D.1. Ask Curr. Coord. to present problem and purchase plan to Supt. and Asst. Supt. for Finance.	Jan. 10, 1997	Curr. Coord.	
E. Get Board of Ed. approval	E.1. Supt. presents plan to Board of Ed.	Feb. Bd. Meet.	Supt.	

Measured Outcomes: Board votes to include cost of security system in district budget for 1997–98 school year.

Ascertain volumes lost in 1996–97 (with no security system). Did high losses continue? Ascertain losses in 1997–98 (with security system). Did loss decrease? By how much?

of some highly technical jargon, and the phrase "measurable outcomes." For our purposes here, we can simply ask ourselves what we want to happen to whom.

MEASURING RESULTS

We cannot completely ignore the "measurable" part, however, because at the end of the plan we want to know in general terms if the plan worked. It is not necessary to get involved in statistical analysis. Here are some examples of goals, all of them with public relations implications:

- Increase the number of teachers who involve the media specialist in instruction-unit planning. The more teachers use the media center, the more students will use it.

At the end of the year compare the number of teachers who planned with you this year to the number from last year.

- Communicate with the principal on a regular basis to discuss media center issues. Regular communication keeps the principal informed about goals, needs, and accomplishments of the media center program.

Did you follow your plan and send the flyers and reports, and hold the meetings planned?

- Increase fiction reading among students (or perhaps among just sixth graders). Promoting reading for pleasure among youngsters pays off in terms of improved reading skills and expands the use of the media center.

Compare this year's circulation figures for fiction to last year's.

Once you have set your goal(s), decide what activities will help get you there. Will you meet monthly with the principal and send reports periodically, have social gatherings in the library media center for teachers, develop a video to show to parents on Open School Night?

Indicate in your plan who will do what. You may have parent volunteers who, after discussions with you, can design and mount attention-getting bulletin boards and display cases. Or perhaps you do the design and leave it at that point for someone else to finish. Students, library aides, other people in the building may have talents and skills you can call on. No matter how many helpful people you have, however, the major responsibility for activities falls on you.

Decide when each activity should be done. Include public relations activities on your planning calendar or daily plan book so they can be worked into your overall schedule. When an activity is accomplished, write in the completion date on your plan.

Evaluate your plan of activities as you move through the year. Did you overestimate the number of articles you could do for the school newspaper? Were some of the flyers you sent nothing to be proud of? Perhaps you need to shift jobs among your helpers. Maybe you should sign up for a workshop at next year's professional conference on how to produce better materials. What feedback are you discerning on your efforts? Do you find the wastebasket next to the teachers' mailboxes full of your flyers, distributed earlier that day, or do teachers rush in to request materials you had put on the flyer distributed only last period?

Your plan is not carved in stone, so you will find it legitimate, and actually necessary, to make adjustments and changes as you move through the time period of your plan. Evaluation is an ongoing function, and changes made in the midst of the plan correspond to route changes as you travel toward your destination on a trip.

At the end of your plan, examine it. Some activities may not have been accomplished. Were they important? Might they have made a difference in the outcome? Why did they not get done? Was your plan too ambitious? Did you give up because time pressures were just too great? Most important, however, did you reach your goal? Did you get where you wanted to go?

BEYOND THE PUBLIC RELATIONS PLAN

Although a formal public relations plan involving special efforts is essential to the achievement of specific advocacy goals, we must also consider ongoing, everyday, interpersonal-relations efforts that influence how the library media center program is perceived as the foundation of our total program.

THE IMAGE PROBLEM

The image of the library media center and of the people who work there is a major factor to deal with when we discuss media center public relations. "Image" is a topic frequently seen on programs at professional conferences and is much in evidence in library literature. In some schools, the library media center is considered by students to be an "uncool" place. Student volunteers may be looked down on by their peers for hanging out there. Indeed, students are sometimes surprised to learn that library media specialists are members of the faculty and not some subspecies. Funding for the media center may suffer if administrators see it as a place unrelated to the instructional program of the school. These attitudes present real hurdles for us, and we must constantly work to change them.

We may be, and most of us are, wonderful, dedicated people doing a magnificent and worthy job under perhaps trying circumstances. Perhaps it is true that nobody understands us. Recommendation number one in a course of action to correct the image problem is to stop whining and examine possible reasons why we don't always get the respect and attention we deserve.

Nobody likes an appreciation-seeking complainer. Decrying our circumstances and wringing our hands make us the very people we do not want to be. Think: Who would want to be around us? Who would put serious funds into the hands of people like that? Whining is not good public relations. And it doesn't work. Of course, you and I never whine, but we know people who do, and it is not a pretty sight.

GAINING RECOGNITION FOR LIBRARIES

So how do we gain recognition, respect, and support for ourselves, our coworkers, and the job we do? We do not lie down and let students walk over us. We do not allow those few teachers who may think we have the cushiest job in the world to use us as doormats. *Never* do we let administrators get the idea that we are baby-sitters on whom they can dump a study hall. We don't confuse being an open, nice, friendly, helpful person with being a pushover. We feel empowered by our skills, and we convey this.

Here are a few suggestions to deal with image problems—those concerning you as well as the media center. All of them make for positive public relations.

The Library Media Center (LMC)—A Comfortable Place to Be

— Change posters, bulletin boards, and displays often.

— Solicit suggestions from students, teachers, and administrators for additions to the collection.

— Purchase some periodicals for fun reading that are not indexed.

— Weed from the collection all the outdated, tattered materials taking up shelf space. This is part of your job. Be ruthless: Get rid of those books where every family is pictured as a blonde mother (with an apron), a father wearing a suit and tie, and there are one boy, one girl, and one dog. Be sure to discard *Asbestos, Man's Best Friend* and all those books about landing on the moon some day.

— Circulate everything.

— Even good ideas get old. Don't let things become static. Be alert to new, better ways of doing things.

Your LMC Staff

— Maintain a sense of humor.

— Be considerate of others, but be assertive about the appropriate role of the library media program and the resources you need to make it outstanding.

— Maintain discipline in a firm but fair manner. People tend to react the way they are treated. If you're aggressive, they're aggressive.

— Don't answer questions with "No." Instead say, "This afternoon is booked solid with classes, but I can schedule your class on Monday." Be firm, but friendly. In a helpful mode, explain briefly to a teacher why he can't bring in a class without advance notice.

— Smile. Even when someone asks if you had to go to college to do your job.

— Volunteer to serve on building and district committees. You are a professional educator.

— Be an active member of your local, state, and national library media association.

— Continue to maintain your sense of humor.

— Don't allow yourself to spend school time (hiding out) in the back room no matter how much you want to get away from it all or how much paper work you have to do.

— Become the best teacher in your school.

— Don't take yourself too seriously, but take your job, your mission, your users very seriously.

— Be a little outrageous—or maybe a whole lot.

— Approach people and offer your help. Sitting at your desk and being available is not enough, no matter how friendly you look.

— Be creative in developing your budget, your schedule, the furniture arrangement, everything.

— Don't try to do everything all the time.

— Create plans for specific purchases (following the planning guide, of course), or groups of purchases, indicating how they fit into the curriculum projects in the school.

— Don't ever apply for just a chunk of money. Present a plan and instructional-oriented justification for everything.

— Establish some personal "trademarks"—gorgeous Indian jewelry, some clothes made of exotic material from some foreign countries you've been to (or brought you by a friend). Every day wear a different button or pin promoting libraries or reading. Of all the things you wear, however, your expression is the most important.

— Impress upon your staff, both paid and volunteer, that they have an important role to play in creating and maintaining a good image for the library media center. Show them how.

— It pays for you to be perceived as accepting and caring. It rubs off on people around you, and it is good for your health. But—you actually should be accepting and caring.

— Keep smiling.

Dealing with Students, Faculty, and Administrators

— Treat students with respect, even when you would prefer to punch their lights out.

— Go into classrooms to teach some of your classes so students see you in a classroom setting. Some of them may think you sleep in the media center. Let people know that you go to parties, vacation in glamorous places, and even go to—or play in!—ball games and other sports events now and then.

— Have live concerts in the media center from time to time. There are probably lots of student musicians in your school, and everybody needs a change of pace now and again.

— Purchase CDs and tapes that students will enjoy.

— From time to time, visit with a group of teachers without mentioning the library center or new materials. You are capable of thinking about and conversing about something other than the media center. You do have a life and a wide variety of frivolous as well as intellectual interests.

— Eat lunch with other teachers and vary your lunch period so that over time you see them all.

— Participate in the social life of the school. Always saying you're too busy and have no time does not impress people with your earnestness and dedication. They simply see you as a dull, stand-offish workaholic.

— Do everything you can to be an active, visible member of the faculty.

— Attend subject-department and grade-level meetings.

— Know the name, classroom location, and courses taught by every teacher in your building.

— Shower administrators with information about what is going on with students in the library media center. Did you learn about GASSING (Getting the Attention of Supervisors) in graduate school?

— Now and then talk to the principal only about positive things. Don't ask for anything.

RESPONSIBILITY FOR PUBLIC RELATIONS

As the library media specialist, you shoulder the chief responsibility for public relations. You are the person who develops and coordinates the master plan and sees to it that all the other staff members are doing their parts. You are the person who must train your staff in how to conduct good public relations with their various, different circles of publics.

But you know what? Everyone on the library media staff bears some responsibility for PR, and there is an unpleasant tendency among those who have a little power to flaunt it. When they have the opportunity to deny permission, they will do so with great vigor and apparent pleasure. Such people must be made to understand that in so doing they are doing real harm to the library media program.

The circulation desk is where this negative behavior is most often observed: "No, you cannot take out that book!" "No, encyclopedias do not circulate." Saying "no" is the only power they have, and they love to throw it around. This need to exercise power is widespread, and it can be found among staff members at all levels. Paid support staff as well as student and community volunteers fall prey to this very human failing. Though it is not widely acknowledged, even some media specialists have been known to act at times in an imperious manner. Any tendency in this direction that we observe in ourselves must be curbed at once. As we train others to weed the word "no" from their conversations with media center users, we too must take the message to heart.

VOLUNTEERS AND PR

There may be volunteer members of the staff who are power hungry and officious and who do not take easily to behavior modification. Assign these people to jobs in the back room. As valuable as most volunteers are to us, we must recognize that in public relations, some people do us more harm than good. Get them away from our customers, the media center users. Perhaps if you ask them to dust shelves, explaining, of course, how important that job is, they will decide to volunteer in someone else's department. Thank them heartily for their services and give them a small gift when they leave. This is good public relations in the long run. Fortunately, few volunteers fall into this damaging group.

There is a more positive side to the care and feeding of most adult volunteers. They can be a source of valuable support for the library media program among their friends and neighbors in the community. They are in a position to see the work that goes on with teachers and kids and to participate in activities in the media center. They can let other community members know what a great job you and the library staff do in the instructional program in the school. They often come to feel an ownership of the media program and partnership with the library media specialist. These people can be a crucial factor in our public relations effort.

A COMFORTABLE ATMOSPHERE

We should give thanks daily that gone forever are the days when library rules required students to come quietly into the room, select a book or magazine, and sit without talking or moving about until the bell rang. Today, in our efforts to maintain an atmosphere of purposeful activity, it is sometimes necessary to curb youthful enthusiasms perhaps better carried out in the cafeteria, the gym, the playing field, or the back seat of a car. Dealing with such difficult situations can be done in a manner that is assertive and firm but not angry. Library staff members need to know who has the authority to discipline students; chances are, it is yours. When you are not in the room or are teaching a class, however, the chore falls to your staff, and they must be aware of how to handle the situation. Yes, how we handle discipline in the library media center is a public relations matter.

We want students, teachers, and administrators to use our services. We want them to see our space as a place in which to work, to learn, to spend their free time. We want them to be comfortable in approaching us for help (hang a sign over your desk reading "Please Interrupt"), for answers to their questions, for suggestions in conducting their research, as well as for the titles of good books to read for pleasure. Perhaps they just want a few minutes to chat with an understanding adult. Behaving in a considerate, caring, knowledgeable manner will attract users to us. Exhibiting the opposite behavior will drive them away. A well-thought-out public relations program that ignores such subtleties as the atmosphere in the library media center and the personalities and attitudes of the media specialist and staff is doomed before the first PR activity is carried out. Recognizing the importance of these intangible aspects of public relations is essential.

Think back to meetings, conferences, or informal gatherings where you met someone or heard a speaker whom you remembered after having had only one contact. Ask yourself, "What was it about Megan Carter that sticks in my mind? Why do I remember this woman whom I've met or heard on only one occasion?"

People who are experts in this field tell us that we make impressions on people and influence them through four channels:

- what we do
- how we look
- what we say
- how we say it.

If we want to influence people to support and use libraries, we should firmly fix in our minds these four channels and how they can work for us in our public relations efforts.

Chapter 1

YOURSELF:
BLOW YOUR OWN HORN,
BECAUSE PR BEGINS WITH YOU

The image many people have of the librarian is that of a meek, shy, retiring woman (despite the number of men who are members of the profession). This image may have come about because at one time many more women than men were librarians, and many women were taught to be modest about their accomplishments. Although this feature of training young women has changed somewhat, the society in which we live still socializes women to feel that if they say good things about themselves, they are in some way putting other people down or "showing off" and being competitive. Women often respond to compliments with embarrassment and dismissive remarks that deflect praise. This societal training sometimes makes it difficult for women to accept compliments and share recognition with others. Men are not the recipients of such training, and most do not seem to be afflicted by the problem, but even male librarians tend to underrate the power inherent in their work and thus their own status in the school community.

SHARE THE GOOD NEWS

Some women are uncomfortable going counter to advice that says that ladies should be self-effacing and maintain a low profile. Many librarians may not only be reluctant to speak well of themselves but also may not be fully aware of how important their work is. Learning to share information about professional accomplishments and successes is something women, as well as many men, have to learn. As a library school professor once said, "He who tooteth not his own trumpet, his trumpet shall not be tooted" (Butler 1990).

None of us, of course, wants to hear someone go on at length about how wonderful he is, what incredible things she has done, how highly esteemed he is, how she can walk on water! (It is a constant source of wonderment to me that such odious persons manage to survive long enough to accomplish so much without being bashed by listeners who simply couldn't take it any longer.) Self-aggrandizement is not good public relations; genuine pride in doing important work well, however, can be very good and compelling public relations. It demonstrates our impact on the big picture of youth development, education, and the nation's social and economic well-being.

It is important to an individual's sense of self-worth to receive praise and recognition. It is equally important that we let our teaching colleagues and administrators know that we are well thought of by others in our field. It is possible, however, to be so assertive that one slips over the line and becomes what appears to be an all-knowing loudmouth. In putting ourselves forward we are not on a giant ego trip. If colleagues are to accept us as equal partners in the educational enterprise, they should know that we have the credentials to fill that role. Let the people you work with know that you have your own areas of specialization, and that it is useful to them and to students to involve you in their planning and teaching. We are experts in our field who are recognized as such by our peers; testimony from outside the building or district reinforces our claims to equal partnership.

Sharing the good news about recognition for achievements makes you feel good; it is also good for your media center program, the school you work in, and for your district. It is proper to keep your administrators up-to-date, and to send news releases to the appropriate media. Blowing your own horn may not be easy for you, but remember, the tune you are playing is not for your own glory but for the good of your media program and your school. Below are some tunes you may want to play.

CREDENTIALS AND HONORS

- Mount on the wall in your office your diplomas, degrees, certificates, and any other paper credentials you have. Have you noticed that you always see degrees on the walls of physicians' and attorneys' offices? They didn't get there by accident. They send nonverbal messages to everyone who enters their offices. It is important that everyone who comes into your space knows that you have the credentials to be an equal partner with your classroom-teacher colleagues.

- Mount on your wall any plaques or honors you have received from your college, your professional organizations, or any group that singles you out for special recognition. Awards offer visibility and proof of professional accomplishment. When these honors are bestowed on you, let your building and district administrators know that one of their staff members has been selected for an honor. Send them photocopies of the citation. Do not be shy about sending news releases to the district newsletter, the student newspaper, and the local newspaper. This is excellent PR for your library media center and your school.

- When you go to Washington, DC, or to your state capital to talk with elected officials about library legislation, have your picture taken with the legislators. Use the photo in a news release when you get back home, and frame a copy for your office. In the write-up accompanying the photo, briefly explain your visit, the topics discussed, and how the lawmakers responded to you. Report on your meeting to your administrators. Your ability to speak with legislators about library issues increases your credentials.

PROFESSIONAL ACTIVITIES

- When you are elected to an office or appointed to a committee in your professional organization, tell the school administrators and send out news releases to the appropriate media. Include in the news release information about the organization, its mission, the size of the membership, and some description of your function in the organization. Don't look at this as taking glory for yourself but rather as making administrators and others aware that they have hired someone whose leadership abilities have been recognized by professional peers beyond the boundaries of the school district.

- Hone your skills as a speaker not only to fellow professionals but also to decision makers and other lay people.

- Inform your administrators when you are invited to speak at a meeting or conference or to present a workshop. Your professional peers have recognized your authority in the field by asking you to share your expertise with them. Include in your memo to the administrators information about the meeting, its purposes, attendance, and something about your presentation.

- Write for publication. The publication of letters to the editors of professional journals, short items solicited by journals on various library media matters, and full-length articles all show that you know your field and that you share your professional knowledge with others. In your writing, remember to identify yourself as a library media specialist in your school district. Make photocopies for administrators and include information about the publication.

PROFESSIONAL GROWTH

- Become an expert grant writer. Attend programs at professional conferences, sign up for a course at your local college, or take an in-service course in writing grant proposals. Seek outside funding for the library media program from foundations, corporations, and local organizations. Offer to guide others in your building through the labyrinthine procedures for obtaining grants. Advertise to your administrators that you are able to bring outside funding into your program, your building, your district. Such successes are real feathers in your cap and a public relations plus for your media center.

- Join your professional organizations and be an involved member. Attend conferences, even if you must pay your way. Be sure to attend any public relations workshops. Professional growth comes through listening to speakers, attending exhibits and workshops, talking with the person sitting next to you in the hotel coffee shop. You come home from conferences physically tired but mentally refreshed and professionally stimulated. You may learn from conversations with other media specialists that your job or your situation is better than you thought. You may come home with new perspectives on your own operation and with ideas about how to deal with some of the less-than-perfect aspects of your professional life. You gain new insights that are valuable to you, your colleagues, your students, and your school. Conference attendance is well worth the time it takes to plan for your absence, the cost of attending, and the time you spend catching up on your return. Do it!

- Write a brief report to your administrator immediately upon returning home from the conference. Highlight some of the programs that you attended, some of the benefits that you gained from attending, some of the great things you saw in the exhibit area, and even some of the disappointments (this gives balance to your report and indicates you have seriously evaluated the experience). Show how some of the programs will specifically benefit you and the students and teachers you work with. Thank your administrator for having approved your request for release time to go to the conference. If the school district paid some of your expenses be especially grateful, since fewer and fewer districts do so. Bring back from vendors in the exhibit area freebies (posters, pencils, paper pads, etc.) for your administrators and your colleagues.

- Become a "techie": when teachers and administrators need electronic information retrieval and speedy communication, make them think automatically of the library media center. Hartzell recommends moving into "the fast lane on the . . . information superhighway as quickly as you can" (Hartzell 1994, p. 156). Hold workshops to train adults in the building in the use of the fax machines, the computers and databases, the Internet, and other electronic resources. The "technologically challenged" will appreciate how you demystify electronic resources and bring them up to speed. You become the expert.

- Get to know the people at the state education department who deal with library media programs. Consult them for advice, help in solving problems, or for sources of professional information. Suggestions, information, and reports about library media matters from state education department consultants sometimes carry authority in the school district beyond that which you have.

- Volunteer to participate in pilot projects, curriculum development projects, and other plans initiated by the library media department of your state education department. Your participation at the state level is good PR for your school district and provides opportunities for professional growth for you.

- Sign up for a "Library Advocacy NOW!" workshop at an ALA conference or at your state association conference. You'll learn from the experts the details on how to get people to support libraries.

MAKE YOURSELF KNOWN

- Have business cards printed with your name, title, school address, and your phone, fax, and E-mail numbers. Use them freely. If your school district provides business cards for administrators, be sure to get them. If the district doesn't, pay for them yourself. It is money well spent . . . and it's tax-deductible!

- You are the authority in your school district on a broad range of topics: books and other materials for particular age groups; the organization of information; materials appropriate for specific units of instruction; databases; off-campus sources of information. This listing only scratches the surface of your expertise. Speak up when your knowledge will be useful; let others know that you are available and willing to be involved in many different ways.

- Strive to increase your visibility in your school and in your district by establishing friendly relationships with a broad range of staff members. You want your colleagues to be familiar with you and to respect and like you. A pleasant atmosphere in the workplace and a coterie of cordial coworkers increase productivity and an all-around sense of job satisfaction. It also helps to have allies who will support you and the library media program even as you support them and their departments.

- Make sure that students know who you are. Many students assume that anyone who works in the library is a librarian. They should understand who the library media specialist is, and that it is that person whom they should consult when they need help doing their research.

- Be sure that your photo is in the faculty section of the student yearbook—not with the photographs of secretaries, custodians, and cafeteria employees. As soon as possible after you are hired, examine the yearbooks. If the librarian is pictured with the faculty, very good, but if not, immediately speak with the student editors, the faculty yearbook advisor, and send a note to the principal about where your picture should be placed in the yearbook and why it should be there: you are a member of the faculty!

- Make sure that your staff is clear on what questions they can answer and which ones they should send to you. You are the media specialist!

- The next time your principal puts out a notice calling for volunteers to serve on regional accreditation teams, sign up. You bring back from school-evaluation visits new ideas, and you see your own media center with a new perspective. When the time comes for an evaluation of your own school, you will have inside knowledge about how visiting teams work and what they look for.

MANAGE STRESS

Learn to control the stress in your life. A day in the life of a library media specialist is seldom the one of peace and quiet so often visualized by the uninitiated. The nature of the job is such that we are often overcome by stress and emotional and physical exhaustion. Students and staff constantly demand our attention; we search for time to prepare and teach classes, to meet and plan with teachers, to perform the many functions our jobs require; we lack clerical help; professional support is sometimes missing; disruptive students create problems; we are unable to see any release in the near future from these pressures.

Ignoring stress can result in both physical and mental problems, and it certainly affects how we feel about our jobs and the people we work with. There are, however, some stress-management techniques we can incorporate into our day:

- Take time to talk to a friend.

- Find time in your schedule to relax, even for five minutes, and think quiet, pleasant thoughts.

- Exercise. A brisk walk around the building at lunch time will calm your mind.

- Drink lots of water and reduce your caffeine intake.

- Try not to let small things bother you.

- Breathe deeply.

- Think positively.

- Accept the situations you cannot change.

- Maintain your sense of humor.

YOUR IMAGE

- It is not easy to change the image of the media specialist, so you need to be careful to avoid perpetuating negative perceptions in the current generation of students. But image relates to much more than personal style and appearance. We need to project ourselves as leaders with vision, confidence, and infectious enthusiasm. This becomes the image of all librarians that youngsters will carry with them throughout their lives.

- Body language is important. If you wear your "don't-you-dare-ask-me-one-more-question" face, they won't then—and they won't on days when you are feeling especially helpful. Most of the media center users don't know much about you personally, and you do not want them to think you were a lion tamer or a prison guard before you became a media specialist. The image you are striving for is one of genuine interest, helpfulness, and approachability.

- Always do more than your job calls for. The sad truth is that people who do only what is required of them do not get noticed, or if they do so it is in a negative way. The extra things you do (e.g., committee service) are good investments in building relationships with administrators and your classroom-teacher colleagues.

Chapter 2

STUDENTS:
WHAT WE'RE ALL ABOUT

It is rumored that there exist some media specialists who think that the purpose of library media programs is to provide them with jobs. Such people should be stripped of their positions and sent back to whatever rock they crawled out from under. Students are our reason for being. They are the key stockholders in our enterprise. The library media programs we develop and put in place are for the benefit of kids. Our teaching passes on to them skills in effectively using information and the library media center and empowers them to become lifelong learners. The planning and consulting we do with teachers integrates information and information-locating skills into subject areas in order to expand student learning. We select and make accessible materials and equipment to benefit the students in our particular buildings and to meet the particular needs of our curriculum. When we encourage reading for pleasure, we help our students develop the joy of reading and learning.

To encourage reading for pleasure we provide books, newspapers, and magazines that are appropriate for their ages and reading levels. We mount bulletin boards, make book lists, give booktalks, and hold reading contests. We cooperate with the public library to promote youngsters' leisure-time reading. Why do we do all this? Because there is a clear relation between reading for fun and higher scores on reading tests: the more youngsters read, the better readers they become. Conversely, students who reduce the time available for reading by watching more television do not score as well on reading tests.

When we work to gain and maintain support for library media centers, we are working to ensure programs that will increase students' educational benefits and achievements. Everything we do should be with students in mind.

THE "SO-WHAT FACTOR" (WHAT'S IN IT FOR KIDS?)

A professor of educational administration told his graduate students to ask themselves constantly, "So what's in it for kids?" This is a question that we should always hold in our minds in case we ever forget for even a moment that we are in a position that is student centered. We can call this question the "so-what factor." Perhaps we should put signs on our desks or make up bumper stickers to remind ourselves of our purpose.

Not all students are lovable or attractive. Some are not even likable, but all of them should be treated fairly, whether they read "good" literature or nothing but their friends' T-shirts. We must squelch whatever violent emotions arise now and again in us and cope with the lack of cooperation or even passive resistance exhibited by that small group of recalcitrant youngsters. We must accept them all as part of life's rich pageant of personalities. If we overreact to youngsters behaving like youngsters, we may lose the opportunity ever to connect with them. We must develop realistic expectations regarding students' behavior. Even students who dislike teachers on general principle respect those who treat them fairly.

We want students to use library media facilities and services. Many are there because of assignments that require them to come into the media center, but we also want kids to come because it is a pleasant, stimulating place to be: comfortable, good books and magazines to use, interesting music to listen to, on-line services to tap into, an atmosphere of helpfulness and genuine interest in individual students. So what do these pleasurable things have to do with a youngster's education? If a student has a positive attitude toward the media center and the media center staff, she will use its services more often to both her immediate and long-term benefits.

Do not expect students to work in absolute silence. We should be able to accept the noise level that comes with purposeful activity. Those who try to make the media center an extremely controlled place will drive students away and cause their own blood pressure to skyrocket. Try to achieve a happy balance between activity-related noise and movement and an atmosphere where there are few enough distractions to get some work done. This is not always an easy goal to attain.

THE LMC—A HAVEN

Our efforts to encourage student use of the media center include providing a welcoming environment, making available material they will want to use, planning activities of interest to them, making the media center easily accessible, organizing the area so they can locate materials and information, and making ourselves and other staff members approachable. We can also set up interesting places in which to read: an old bathtub padded with colorful pillows, a "tree house" accessible by ladder, or a private reading "room" that was once a telephone booth. Kids love these things.

Many of them also crave the attention and encouragement of a trusted adult who is willing to listen with respect and empathy.

Some of the students we see come from homes that lack caring parents, financial resources, and any kind of stability. Instead they are generously furnished with a high level of frustration, anger, and depression. School is often the only place such children are noticed, the only place they feel welcome and secure, the only place adults listen to them and talk to them. In her study of high-risk children, Emmy Werner found that one of the factors that enabled one child in three to overcome severely adverse aspects of their lives was a tie with a caring adult other than a parent (Werner 1992).

Media centers are often the place in the school where such children feel especially comfortable. There are no grades, no tests, no assigned seats; there is less structure than in the classroom, and the media specialist often takes time to chat with a child, gives the young person a chance to be helpful, focuses some special, individual attention available nowhere else in the child's life. The media specialist can be an adult friend, and the library media center can come to be the only warm, safe world the student can rely on.

STUDENT VOLUNTEERS

When you publicize the need for student volunteers, you will probably get a good response. Indeed, often students come to the librarian and ask if there are jobs they can do. Many of these students are those who are not part of other groups—not the academically talented (whose schedules are filled with extra courses and extracurricular activities) or the athletes. They may be marginal students, those at risk, or shy youngsters who have not yet found a comfortable niche. They may be students who like books and reading, working with computers, or dealing with instructional equipment. Being a part of the library media volunteer staff provides them with a group to belong to and opportunities to increase their self-esteem, and opens the door for them to learn how to carry out responsibilities and do a good job. Some of the tasks that student volunteers can do are: handle equipment, process and arrange materials, and help others.

HANDLE EQUIPMENT

- Train student volunteers to operate instructional equipment. When teachers have problems, the student on duty can deal with it. Award operators' licenses at special awards ceremonies. Be sure that photos are taken and that the write-up gets into the school newspaper as well as the local newspaper. The same, of course, applies to computers.

- The students can be responsible for delivering equipment to classrooms and collecting it at the end of the day.

PROCESS MATERIALS

Students can be assigned to:

- property-stamp new materials
- fold and put materials in envelopes for mailing
- send for tourist information from state tourist agencies
- send for college catalogs.

ARRANGE MATERIALS

Ask the students to:

- look through local newspapers and clip articles for the bulletin board about the school and students in the school
- keep the paperback book collection in order, repair torn covers, replace spine labels
- be responsible for keeping a section of shelves in order
- check in and file microfiche
- keep the college catalog collection in order, discarding old issues and inserting new ones
- put newspapers on sticks.

HELP OTHERS

This is a great way to help a student's self-esteem. Make them responsible for:

- photocopying materials teachers have left to be done
- helping other students and teachers use computers
- giving tours of the media center to parents on Open House Night
- demonstrating to parents on Open House Night how to use computers and other equipment
- greeting visitors at the building entrance and conducting them to the media center when you have a meeting attended by people outside your building.

STUDENTS AS LIBRARY ADVOCATES

Students who have positive experiences in the media center can become spokespersons for the media center program at budget hearings and at board of education meetings. Testimony provided by our satisfied customers often carries a great deal of weight with decision makers in our school districts. Reaching out to students is a great way to reach parents whose opinions and attitudes about the schools are based largely on what their youngsters tell them. In this way students help us, unconsciously, achieve the cooperation and support we need from the community.

Students can also be effective speakers in the cause of library media centers in legislators' offices at the state capitol and in Washington, D.C. Students from several states were official delegates to the White House Conference on Library and Information Services in 1991, where they spoke enthusiastically about the importance of library services in their lives and helped achieve top priority status for the recommendations on improving youth services in libraries, both school and public.

Parents consider students the best source of information about schools (Dierksen and Oberg 1981). For example, when asked to identify their top school information source, 77 percent of parents of seventh graders picked their children over teachers, newsletters, or reports. When parents ask, "What went on in school today?" for better or for worse, students tell them much about teachers and class work that shapes parents' opinions and perceptions.

As you look over the following suggestions of ways to promote the library media center and make it attractive to the students in your school, keep in mind the "so-what factor" and how students can serve as a public relations medium. A successful public relations program "will create a citizenry that will hold libraries in high esteem and support them at every level" (Saretsky 1991, p. 74).

DISPLAYS ATTRACT STUDENTS

- Get some volunteers—students, teachers, parents—to help you make a life-sized, soft doll to arrange in different ways and in varying costumes in the media center. Name it Melville or Melvilla Dewey.

- Borrow a skeleton from the biology teacher and have it reading a spooky book in a Halloween display.

- Acquire a mannequin and dress it in a school sports uniform, as a character from a book, or as a librarian (yourself) in your clothing. Change the costume to match the season of the year or a particular display. Set it up in interesting circumstances—perhaps lounging on the card catalog reading a book, reading on skis.

- Take photos of each media center staff member, volunteer, and student helper and arrange them on a bulletin board or display case. Under each picture list the person's name and title and a few of her or his responsibilities. Make sure that you list at least one humorous chore for each person (e.g., makes all the really important decisions; selects the books dealing with quantum physics; sets and empties the mousetraps; answers all questions about flights to Vail). This is good to use early in the school year so students new to the building can learn who staff members are, and returning students will be reminded of names. It also points out that not everyone who works in the media center is a media specialist, a distinction that many students (like many adults) are not aware of.

- Take photos of bulletin boards and display cases and keep them in a scrap book. The ideas can be adapted every few years.

- Do a bulletin board or display case on short books. Get teachers to approve short books for some book reports.

- Do a bulletin board and bibliographies on "Books to Read if You Don't Like to Read."

- Set aside one bulletin board in the media center on which to post articles and pictures of students that have appeared in the town, school, or district newspaper or newsletter. Ask a volunteer or student helper to keep it current.

- Take instant photos of various students for a bulletin board or display case. Ask each one to name his or her favorite type of reading—*Car and Driver*, any novel by V. C. Andrews, the sports pages, *Vogue*, or whatever. Put the person's name and favorite reading on a label and attach to the picture. You can include faculty, custodians, administrators, everyone on this display. Kids love to see pictures of themselves and their friends and may be surprised to know who reads what.

- Some night when you can't sleep, begin a list of 101 wonderful things to do in the library media center. Include along with the traditional things (such as read the comics; look up Ashurbanipal in the *Biographical Dictionary*; use an atlas to find out where Azerbaidzhan is located) some others such as: take a nap; bug the librarian; etc. If you can't think of 101 then let it be 67, or however many you can come up with (see Figure 2–1).

- Next, take instant photos of kids, teachers, and others doing these things and label each with the person's name and the activity (kids love to see pictures of themselves). Mount with the heading ("101 Wonderful Things . . . ") on a bulletin board. If you have a hall display case, so much the better. There you can reach people who don't usually come into the media center. Students not pictured will come to you asking to have their pictures taken.

- This attention-getting display can also showcase services, activities, and materials people may not be aware of. And the list itself makes a good handout.

Figure 2–1 Wonderful Things List

Several More than 101 Wonderful Things to Do in the Library Media Center

Read a newspaper.
Get hints on making movies.
Watch a videotape.
Learn to play chess.
Listen to a story.
Count the books in the library.
Choose a book to read to your little sister.
Borrow Hawaiian music for your luau.
Look up a number in the phone book.
Gaze at an art reproduction.
Use a video camera.
Ask the librarian a hard question.
Return your overdue books.
Read about the birds and the bees.
Write a love letter.
Write a letter of complaint.
Copy plans for making a bird house.
Analyze your handwriting.
Water the plants.
Listen to the plants grow.
Apply for a job.
Learn to identify poison ivy.
Read Lincoln's papers on microfilm.
Solve a crossword puzzle.
Teach yourself to knit.
Take an armchair trip to India.
Brush up your Shakespeare.
Look up today's skiing conditions in Vail.
Catch up on your Zs.
Find the population of Paris.
Ponder the meaning of life.
Get warm.
Get cool.
Get smart.
Find out where to go canoeing.
Read the graffiti.
Request a book from another library.
Feed the fish.
Prepare for your SATs.
Find out who your congressperson is.
Find out who won yesterday's game.

Find an article on buying a lawn mower in *Reader's Guide*.
Plan a trip to Florida.
Look at a slide of a smoker's lungs—yuk!
Ask the librarian to get more books on sky-diving.
Find out the seven signs of cancer.
Locate a recipe for roasting a pig.
Bug a librarian.
Hug a librarian.
Learn who won the World Series in 1972.
Find Elvis's birthday.
Read the want ads.
Learn how to repair your transmission.
Make a list of good restaurants in your county.
Write a poem.
Explore African American culture.
Use the yellow pages.
Compare brands of peanut butters in *Consumer Reports*.
Get the facts from Masters and Johnson.
Request a magazine article from a neighboring high school library.
Learn to play the zither.
Hunt up the rules for playing korfball.
Learn who starred in *Casablanca*.
What other movies did they appear in?
Learn to bake a chocolate cake.
Learn to train your dog.
Learn to read better and faster.
Find the words to "The Good Ship Lollypop."
Read the *N.Y. Times* for Monday, December 8, 1941.
Find out how to view an eclipse safely.
Learn the dates of National Pickle Week.
Find out what "egregious" means.
Look up a synonym for "egregious."
Find out what the "A" stood for in *The Scarlet Letter*.
Settle an argument.
Look up your senator's voting record.
Locate your house on a city map.
Use *Current Biography* to learn about Janet Reno.

Figure 2–1 (cont.)

Check on how to write a footnote.
Research Civil War uniforms.
Read a review of the movie *Fargo.*
Prepare a speech for Mr. O'Neill's class.
Watch other people work.
Identify a snake you saw in your yard yesterday. *Do not* bring the snake to the library!
Make a list of ways to save the Earth.
Arrange to borrow a reference book overnight.
Choose a book to read for your English class.
Speak to the librarian in French.
Discover another culture.
Read a Maya Angelou poem.
Borrow a large-print book for your grandmother.
Contemplate your future in the peace and quiet.
Make a list of "new" European countries.
Get some ideas about what to wear to the prom.
Get a date for the prom.
Thank the library aides for their help.
Learn how to reduce stress in your life.

Use Reserve books for Mr. Cash's class.
Borrow markers to make a birthday card.
Look over the New Book Display for a really good read.
Learn how to be a more successful student.
Plan a week's menus to reduce fat in your diet.
Reserve a copy of a book that's checked out.
Learn about a career as a forest ranger.
Help put up a bulletin board.
Borrow a camera to take to a party.
Look up your Aunt Debbie in *Who's Who.*
Check Dow Jones to see how your stocks are doing.
Learn what else happened on the day you were born.
Look through the yearbook for the year your Dad graduated.
Do your homework.
Read.
Ask the librarian for 101 more things to do in the library.

- "How to Study" is a good topic for display. Gather the books you have on effective studying techniques and prepare flyers and bookmarks listing tips (see Figure 2–2). Parents may like to see this at Open House time.

- Change your bulletin board (before it becomes bulletin bored), display case, posters, supply of bookmarks, etc., often and avoid the Miss Havisham syndrome.

STUDENTS AND PAPERBACKS

- Purchase lots of paperbacks in multiple copies and arrange them the way bookstores do, so the covers face out. Students will be more likely to pick up books when the covers are visible. Who says you can't tell a book by its cover?

- Place paperback racks near the circulation desk the way supermarkets do the *National Enquirer.* It certainly works for them.

- Make a list of paperback reference books that students might find useful to own. Send copies of the list home to parents.

Figure 2–2 Bookmark Topics

Design bookmarks for special times of the year using an appropriate picture and listing four or five book titles.

Martin Luther King Day
Banned Book Week
American Education Week
Baseball Season Opening
Valentine's Day
Women's History Month
Black History Month
School Library Media Month

Check *Chase's Annual Events* for special weeks and days.

NEW BOOKS AND OLD

- Do some book processing out in the open where students and others can see what's newly arrived. Let users place holds on books they want to read when processing is finished.

- Ask students to help you open and unload boxes of new materials. Give your volunteers first chance to borrow them.

- If you are short of space, you need to weed the collection ruthlessly to free up room for new, up-to-date materials. Give away the discards to whoever wants them. It is surprising what treasures students, teachers, and others find among the things you call junk. Clearly stamp the items "WITHDRAWN" and put them on a cart with a big sign that says, "Freebies! Help Yourself!" Provide recycled paper bags in which they can carry away their finds. My favorite comment came when a student found a book with a 1963 date and joyously declared, "I've found a rare book published before I was born! It's probably worth a lot of money."

WHAT OTHERS HAVE READ

- Leave carts with recently checked-in books where students can see them. Maybe some books will be taken and they won't have to be reshelved.

- Ask students to contribute comments on books they liked in a notebook you keep on the circulation desk. When students ask if you have any good books, let them look through it to see which books their fellow students liked.

KEEP UP WITH KIDS' INTERESTS

- Stay on top of which things are popular with students. Spend some time watching videos, MTV, a popular new movie. Listen to a hot-selling tape or CD. Get student advice on adding some new music selections to the collection as well as some magazines. (Personal experience, however, indicates that we are still not ready for *Playboy*. Details available upon request.) Being cool and identifying with where students are coming from does not necessarily require, however, that you go in for body piercing or have the Dewey Decimal System tattooed on your forehead.

- Place a suggestion box in the media center and make its installation an occasion. Publicize it in the school newspaper and in the PA announcements. Have someone photograph a student dropping in the first suggestion. Let students know that you want their suggestions for purchases (books, magazines, tapes, CDs, etc.), as well as comments on media center policies. Open the box often, and type and mount above the box the suggestions and your responses. You may, of course, have to edit some suggestions.

- Put up a graffiti board and encourage students to write on it. If they get it out of their systems here they may write fewer comments on desks, walls, and elsewhere. Develop a thick skin.

- Create a student advisory council. This may grow out of some comment from the suggestion box. The council may advise on purchases; help with ideas to deal with student discipline in the media center; suggest ways to handle graffiti, vandalism, and theft. Warning: advisory councils won't work if you never take their advice.

- Set aside a portion of your book budget and let students choose books to purchase. Provide them with reviews from which they can make selections. This gives them the opportunity to have some say in their world.

STUDENTS AND TECHNOLOGY

- Arrange for students in your building to communicate by E-mail with students on their grade level across the state to exchange reviews and critiques of books they have read, get to make new friends, and become competent technology users.

- Let students use a computer program to make banners for special events in the library media center. Ask them to color the banners and mount them in the corridor over the media center entrance or in some other prominent spot.

- Ask students to generate award certificates for you using a computer program.

- Assign a student volunteer to produce each morning a printout of the day's weather report from the weather database and to post it on the Keep Current bulletin board.

RULES, ETC.

- Overdue books are a real hangup for students and don't make the media specialist happy, either. Overdue notices are time consuming and not very effective. Experiment with a new circulation period. The traditional two weeks just may not be long enough. Ponder this thoughtfully. You may make some new friends for the media center with a four-week loan period.

- Make a big deal of students who never have overdue or lost books.

- Codify rules for student behavior in the media center. Accentuate the positive. Post rules where they will be obvious, and make sure that students understand them. Be sure that they are included in the school's student handbook.

FUN THINGS TO DO

- If you have the space for it, put out a jigsaw puzzle for kids and teachers to add pieces to.

- Read aloud in the media center every morning before the regular school day begins. Attendance at such a program will depend on how youngsters get to school and how much time they have before school starts.

- If you have space, allow students to play chess and other board games in the media center. It is possible, however, that these supposedly quiet games will turn into contact sports. If they do, put them away for a few months—or maybe forever.

RECOGNITION AND AWARDS

- Place media center logos on T-shirts, baseball-type caps, or patches for jackets to give to student volunteers. If you can come up with the money, go for sweaters, sweatshirts, or windbreaker-type jackets. Students wear (and highly prize) sports letters and clothing. Why not give them recognition for their media center service? Present these at special award ceremonies at a school board meeting, or perhaps at an annual cookout or spaghetti dinner for student volunteers. Ask a building or a district administrator to be the after-dinner speaker and to present the awards. Arrange for media coverage.

- Present library media center achievement or service awards at the school's end-of-year awards ceremony.

- Present graduation gifts to your student volunteers in recognition of their library service. You may want to have an end-of-the-year party to honor them.

- Give special recognition to students who achieve high honors for two consecutive marking periods by awarding them Library Keys, which are special passes to come to the media center. Make a ceremony of presenting the keys and invite parents to attend.

- Write notes to the parents of students who are avid readers. Point out that being a good reader is an indicator of success in school and in later life. Ask a building administrator to sign the letter along with you.

- Establish a "Life Long Learner Award," and bestow it upon a graduating senior who has used the library media center for self-improvement and demonstrated that he or she will continue to be a library user. Ask the Friends of the Library Media Center or some other group to fund this award.

- If your principal asks each subject department to select a Student-of-the-Month, let her know that you want library media included in the activity. Decide on and publicize the criteria for the "Library Media Student of the Month" and include your chosen student with the others.

SPECIAL EVENTS

- Hold competitions several times a year. These can range from identifying the source of a quotation to guessing how many feet of shelving there are in the media center. Advertise in the school newspaper and ask an important school person to present the prize, which might be a gift certificate from a book store or special privileges in the media center. Make it a big thing: photograph the presentation, and proclaim the winners on the daily PA announcements.

- Hold contests in the media center. Ask students to enter their creations, such as cartoons, jokes, posters, or book jackets, and display all entries. Ask teachers and administrators to serve as judges. Advertise in the school newspapers and on the PA. Award prizes and do write-ups for the school paper.

- Plan a library booth, a contest, or an activity for your school's annual carnival.

- Hold a book fair in the library media center. In some areas where there are no book stores, this may be the only opportunity for students to purchase books. Help younger students make discriminating choices. Get adult volunteers to help you.

- Hold a film festival in the library. Choose several short films and run them all day. Invite teachers to schedule classes to come in. Provide popcorn.

- Plan a Young Authors' Celebration in your school. Invite parents and other community members to come to the media center to hear students read from their written works. Ask teachers to join you in organizing this project.

- In cooperation with the art department, hold an annual student art show in the media center. Art students will appreciate having their works displayed, and nonart students will enjoy seeing the works of their friends. One night have an Open House for the community, and be sure to invite local officials, the media, district administrators, and school board members.

- Plan a buildingwide or districtwide project to encourage children to become better readers. For example, Dade County (Florida) Public Schools joined with the United Teachers of Dade County and the Greater Miami Chamber of Commerce to develop the program *Miami Reads . . . All Year Long*. This project grew out of research that indicates that free voluntary reading is the greatest predictor of student success. The planners developed packets targeting elementary, middle, and senior high schools. The packets contained activities designed to support and extend the reading program in the schools and to involve the active participation of parents. Each packet contained reading and writing activities for each month, bulletin board ideas, community-service activities, reading suggestions, and flyers to promote *Miami Reads*.

Two packets went to each school principal, one to be given to the library media specialist and the other to be shared by classroom teachers. Library media specialists attended an in-service session to help them implement the programs in their schools.

- Invent and establish special days or weeks throughout the year in your school. Enlist the support of your principal and the faculty in celebrating with storytelling, reading, writing, drawing, and displays of whatever topic you have chosen. You might celebrate apples or other foods, a particular animal (kangaroos), or a book genre (survival, fairy tales, mythology). Be sure the media center is an important part of the activities and that you participate as well as serve as a resource person.

- When the occasion is appropriate, take one or more students with you to a meeting. They especially enjoy hearing authors talk about their work. Most students have never seen a "real" author, and they come away wanting to read the author's books. Attending a session of this kind helps strengthen the bond with students.

STUDENT-FOCUSED ADVERTISEMENTS

- Ask the editor of the student newspaper to assign a reporter to the media center beat. Keep a list of topics you can bring up in interviews with the reporter, and always have something new or interesting to report. Never indicate that nothing has happened.

- Prepare a short paragraph for the morning PA announcements on special occasions about the importance of the event or occasion (e.g., Women's History Month, Lincoln's Birthday). Always end with, "For more information, visit your library media center." Prepare short bibliographies for these occasions.

- Publish a library media center newsletter on a regular basis. June Muldner produces a monthly newsletter that she distributes to the fourth and fifth grades. Her aim is to increase reading and library use among these youngsters. She includes puzzles, short articles on books and authors, and, in one issue, "If you like the movie, you'll love the book!"—an article in which she suggests book titles on the same topics as popular movies.

- Feature some library media center material in each weekly activity schedule, which is prepared in the school office and posted in the classrooms and around the building. Include a brief review of the material and place it on display at the circulation desk in the media center.

- Purchase advertisements for the library media center in the school's annual drama program, the yearbook, and in other school publications that contain ads. Student will appreciate your support, as will their parents.

ENCOURAGE STUDENT READING

- Prepare short bibliographies on popular topics (e.g., romance, football, skateboarding, family relationships, adventure, horror, survival) in which you include fiction, nonfiction, and magazine articles. Be sure to appeal to all kinds of readers. Design attractive flyers or folders and have them available at various places around the media center. Change them often.

- Make a lot of mobiles on different topics to hang from the ceiling. Each moving part should contain the title of a book and its author. Get students to help you generate the lists as well as the topics they are interested in. Change them often. They look great up in the air.

- If the students in your school ride the school bus, develop a campaign to encourage reading on the bus. The bus driver would probably nominate you for sainthood.

BE HELPFUL

- Remove from your vocabulary the Six Most Dreaded Words, "look it up in the catalog," as an all-purpose response to students' requests. It is legal to point out where the dictionaries are shelved, and you won't be drummed out of the profession if you say, "Yes, we have Judy Blume books. Look in the first paperback rack." We certainly do want students to learn the usefulness of the catalog, but when they come dashing into the library between classes we can provide some shortcuts.

- Decide what time period works for you and then let students check out tape recorders, instant-picture cameras, video cameras, and other equipment for home use. If they are working on projects for class, provide the film or whatever supplies they need. Consider adding their finished products to the permanent media center collection with, of course, a complete entry in the catalogue. (This suggestion is not workable galaxywide, but then neither are other ones in this book!)

- Keep a "cutting stack" of duplicates or discarded copies of magazines. Students frequently need pictures for projects, and making available copies they can cut up may save the current issues.

- Keep a mending kit with needles, thread, and safety pins in your desk for students to use. Place a full-length mirror so ali media center users can check on their appearance.

- Keep at the circulation desk items that students may want to borrow to use in the media center: cellophane tape, pencils, pens, rulers, protractors and compasses, colored pencils, and pens. Ask borrowers to leave an ID card that will be returned when the items are handed back. Warning: loss rate can be high, even with ID cards.

- Purchase a quantity of inexpensive pencils and ballpoint pens printed with the name of the media center. Sell these for a price that covers the cost of the items. (Caveat: some districts do not allow you to sell items, but others do, so check it out.) So, when a student asks to borrow a pencil or pen, say, "I don't have pencils to lend, but I can sell you one for your very own for only five cents." Of course, if your school district allows you to make a small profit, you could apply that profit toward the purchase of paperbacks, newspapers, or other specific items.

- Ask the front office to save for the media center the pencil stubs (four inches or so) left after student testing. These are too short to use again, but are great to put in a box on the circulation desk or the card catalog (if you still have one) and at other handy places. Golf-playing teachers are also good sources for these little pencils. If students don't return them, you've suffered no loss.

- Keep construction paper and felt-tip markers on hand for students to use in making posters or covers for reports.

- During exam week in the high school, when the school is running on an exam schedule, set up the media center as a quiet study area. This may be the only place in the building where students can find a quiet spot to prepare for their next exam. Relaxing, visiting, and hanging out can take place in the cafeteria or some other specific place in the school. The media center during this time becomes a place where students can really concentrate. This sometimes visits a hardship on the staff, however, if they tend to be noisy and distracting.

- Invite your school's honor society to hold its Christmas tea in the library media center. Be sure they do all the work, especially the clean-up.

HAVE STUDENTS ENCOURAGE READING

- Buy some classic elementary-level books for your high school collection. Suggest that students borrow them to read to the youngsters in their families or to their neighbors.

- Develop a library literacy program for the teenage mothers in your high school.

Make sure the young parents know that good readers are good learners. Teach them how to read aloud to their infants and toddlers and how to select quality books that have lasting quality.

- Establish a program for your high-school or middle-school students to visit elementary schools to read to those youngsters.

- Allow student tutors to work with their students in the library media center.

ESL AND EXCHANGE STUDENTS

- Add some high-interest, low-reading-level books to your high-school media collection. Be sure the reading teachers, ESL teachers, and special education teachers know about them.

- Introduce your foreign-exchange students to the wonders of E-mail so they can correspond electronically with friends from their hometowns.

- Consider purchasing a short-wave radio so exchange students and other foreign-language speakers can enjoy hearing other languages. The foreign language department might come up with some funds to help make this project possible.

SIGNAGE

- Take time to walk the corridors of your school looking at signs pointing the way to the media center. Can you get there from here? Check especially at corners, intersections, and stairways. Remedy the situation if there are no signs, or if they are unclear or unattractive.

- Students and other media center users like to be independent. Help them to help themselves by placing signs in strategic places: on the ends of stacks; on equipment explaining how it works; for the reference, magazine, computer, and index areas. Post your operating hours at entrances, and prominently display rules for behavior. Identify where materials are checked out and returned, and where to find new books.

- Put up signs in the media center in every language taught or spoken by students in the school. Have foreign language dictionaries in every one of these languages. ESL teachers may help you locate materials in languages you may never have stocked before. Make the media center a warm, welcoming place for students new to English and to the school.

- Have all media center staff members wear name tags with their titles. Each person should also have a sign on her desk with her name and title. Students seem to be more comfortable if they know names, and it benefits new faculty members, too.

WELCOME NEW STUDENTS

- Prepare a guide to your high-school library media center for incoming ninth graders and other students new to the building. Include information about how the media specialist can help them, the hours the center is open, policies, services available to students, materials in the collection, and a floor plan. You can ask an art teacher to help you design the guide.

- Develop an audiotape tour of the media center that students new to the school can use with a Walkman-type player.

- See Figure 2–3 on the next page for a sample flyer welcoming incoming ninth-graders.

Figure 2–3 Sample Incoming Ninth-Grade Welcome

TO: Incoming Ninth Graders

FROM: Ms. Flowers and Ms. Mulcahy

              B.S.H.S. Librarians

RE: Library Media Services

DATE: May 9, 19—

Welcome to Beech South High School! We were happy to meet some of you in the high school yesterday and especially in the library. Your tour did not allow enough time for you to absorb all the information about the building that will be your school home for the next four years, but we hope that you will find your way to the library early in September.

We have many books, computer databases, magazines, CDs, video- and audiotapes, and other things that will be useful for your class work—as well as just fun things to use. We hope you will want to spend some of your free periods with us each day.

If you have extra time, consider becoming a library volunteer. Ms. Owens and Ms. Walker, your current librarians, tell us that some of you have volunteered in the middle-school library. We always need helpers.

Come look over the high school Library Media Center and what we have to offer you. We can't wait to meet you.

Chapter 3

BUILDING STAFF: ALL MEMBERS OF THE TEAM

FACULTY

Although we always work hard to attract students to the library media center and cherish the one-to-one relationships we have with them, it is perhaps even more important that we develop an excellent rapport with the teachers in our buildings. In working with a teacher we are indirectly giving attention to an entire class or several classes of students. So if you must set priorities, put faculty members at the top of your list. By familiarizing ourselves with what they are teaching and involving ourselves in planning for curriculum changes, we can make an impact on meeting the institutional goals of the school and the education of kids. This doesn't happen if we stay in the back room cataloguing books or inputting data in the computer.

Part of our job is to know the entire curriculum of the school—an awesome task. We are the materials experts in our buildings: we have to know about materials for courses ranging from auto mechanics to zoology; from alphabet books to zither playing. We can learn about new materials and technologies by attending conferences, visiting exhibits, reading reviews, and talking to other media center specialists, but we learn about the curriculum in our buildings from the teachers. It follows then, that our ability to perform our function depends to a large extent on teachers. If we do not have good working relationships with them, we can find ourselves in very deep waters, indeed.

It is difficult to face the fact that the library is not a high priority for everyone, and not all teachers, as well we know, are enamored with the idea of involving us in curriculum design and development. Some of them, especially those long-time laborers in the vineyards, see little advantage in searching for the time to plan jointly with us on resource-based instruction units. We must win them to this concept.

INVOLVE TEACHERS

You and the principal should share the responsibility of making teachers aware of the advantages that will accrue to them if they cooperate with you. The principal who understands the impact that the library media program and the library media specialist have on the learning program in the school will work to develop among teachers an awareness and commitment to planning and teaching with you in a collaborative way.

Not all teachers know how useful library media services can be to them and their students' achievement—some may never have taught in a school with a good library media program. So it is up to us to find ways to get to know the teachers and what they teach and to provide opportunities for them to get to know us, to recognize our expertise, and to learn how we can work together for the educational benefit of kids. Although you may never make media center users of every teacher in your building, chances are you can significantly increase the percentage. Start by attracting teachers into the media center to use the excellent electric pencil sharpener you invested in, or to look over the teachers' association materials you persuaded the TA president to house there, or to refer to the district's policy handbook.

In point of fact, every time a teacher enters the center, she sees books, equipment, software, or a magazine she didn't know about. Speak to as many teachers as you can. Always have some wonderful materials to share, some service to mention. You, the teacher, the materials, and services all synergize to persuade the teacher to use library media services.

Get to know your teachers so well that your computer-like mind immediately connects reviews or new materials with a teacher: "This would be great for Donna's unit on the home front during World War II," or "This is just what George needs when his Latin students work on the Roman Army." These moments, and they come constantly, make our jobs exciting and fun.

In our efforts to win teachers over to the services of the library, we offer to do many things that are not in our job descriptions. They may call for an investment in time and money, but the return on that investment can be enormous. Once teachers come to understand how valuable a partnership with us can be, we will have won not only a media center user but a media center supporter as well. When we do even a small favor for a teacher—supply her with a piece of equipment or software that fills an immediate void, or anticipate what he is going to need—the teacher feels a sense of obligation to us. These teachers are then likely to give us their support when we request it because we have been helpful to them. It is human nature to want to do something for someone who has done something for you.

TEACHERS AS LIBRARY SUPPORTERS

Savvy teachers involve us in their planning, integrate library media resources in their classroom activities, use library media services, and require their students to do so. They know how seriously their teaching would be affected if media center services were reduced, if materials budgets did not grow, or if we were not there full-time to bring it all together.

Teachers can speak in support of media center programs to building and district administrators, to members of the board of education, to decision makers at the state level, and they can write letters to newspapers. Local teachers' associations can press for resolutions to strengthen library media center services in the association's state platform for action. There is power in numbers, and the message coming from media center users statewide is more powerful than it is coming from just us.

Your library media program needs the understanding and support of the teachers in your building in order to be successful, and public relations is vital to ensuring that success. Following are some ideas about how to get teachers into the media center, make them aware of your services, and become better acquainted with them and their needs. Find out which ideas work for you.

WELCOME TEACHERS

- At beginning of the school year, distribute folders containing a welcome to the new school year; information on media center policies; lists of media center services (see Figure 3–1); how to schedule classes into the media center; how to put materials on reserve; lists of periodical subscriptions (see Figure 3–2); lists of holdings in any special collection (e.g., maps, picture sets, posters, on-line services); interlibrary loan services; a fun reading list for teachers; forms; and any other goodies you can think of. Include a note suggesting they save the folders for filing other materials you will be sending during the year. Thereafter, give folders to new teachers as they join the staff.

- Ask the principal for a time slot on her schedule for new teacher orientation. Present new teachers with folders and talk about library services.

- Invite new teachers to drop in for coffee, tea, sympathy, or whatever when they are free. The point here is to make people new to the building feel at home and to establish a working relationship with them as soon as possible.

- Invite faculty members to attend a "Welcome Back to School" breakfast in September in the media center. You can send out an attractive invitation and have new materials and equipment on display.

- Develop a brochure each fall to welcome teachers back to school that sends wishes for a good school year, outlines library media services, media center rules, and other special information.

Figure 3–1 List of Services

LIBRARY MEDIA SERVICES to make
your life easier (our raison d'être):

1. Plan teaching units with you

2. Teach information retrieval skills
   to your classes

3. Make bibliographies for your
   teaching units

4. Send equipment to your classroom

5. Teach you how to use equipment

6. Place materials on reserve for
   your classes

7. Schedule your classes in the library media center to work (under your
   direction) on projects

8. Send you issues of current magazines

9. Photocopy articles of interest to you

10. Tape TV programs for class use

11. Accept recommendations for purchase

12. Brainstorm with you ideas for projects

13. Recommend materials for use with your classes

14. Provide that relaxing cup of tea or coffee

15. Smile and offer a cheery word as you pass by (cheery words Tuesday
    thru Friday only)

16. Inform you of new books, equipment, software, computer services

17. Arrange interlibrary loans for you and your students

18. Talk with you about your needs. We want to work with you!

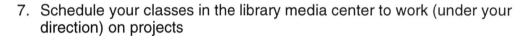

Figure 3–2 Folders for Teachers

To: The Faculty

From: Library Media Center

Re: Library Media Information

Date: January 10

We are pleased to welcome the new year by presenting you with your very own folder (please note *your* name inscribed on the cover) in which to file our communications. Our first contribution to your folder is the attached list of magazines which we are currently receiving. If you would like more specific information about our magazine holdings you may consult the list posted in the library or call us at ext. 235.

Happy New Year!

- Get to know the student teachers who come to your building. Invite them to the media center for an orientation, a tour, and a cup of coffee. Be sure that they (and their mentor teacher) know that media center services are available to them. With help from you they may develop into strong media center supporters when they move on to their first jobs.

SOCIAL INTERACTION

- Hold a Brown Bag lunch in the media center for the faculty during teacher conference days (see Figure 3–3). They bring their lunches, you provide the beverage. Needless to say, you have a wide variety of material on display.

- Send faculty and administrators a brochure announcing School Library Media Month activities in the library media center. Include an early-morning open house specifically for them.

Figure 3–3 Library Luncheon

You are cordially invited to join these illustrious folk for lunch in the library on Tuesday, November 4. The deadline for signing up is *Friday, October 31*. Right now, this minute, send in your response to Flowers, Mulcahy, or Matthews. Don't be left out. You could be dining with:

F. Mauceri	V. Mahr	L. Rossen	R. Hornik	M. Littlefair
S. Orobono	E. Mulcahy	B. Ruter	E. Stiles	F. Champagne
W. Goebel	A. Schwartz	M. Petralia	D. Doran	A. Stern
H. Flowers	C. Harbart	J. Nash	C. Matthews	E. Phipps
P. Veraldo	M. Leddy	E. McEnerny	A. Nadelson	R. Rosener
P. Ponzi				

____ Save a space for me.

____ My $4.00 is attached.

____ I'll pay on Monday, November 3.

Your name _____

- Display holiday craft books at appropriate times of the year, and send holiday greetings.

- Take your lunch period every day and eat in the lunch room with the other teachers. There are media specialists who say they are much too busy to eat lunch. This is not good PR. For one thing, it sounds whiny, like "Poor, overworked, put-upon me. I never have time for lunch." If your school has several lunch periods, vary the period you go to lunch so you see different teachers. Mention special materials you have received that were requested by a particular teacher, but don't limit your conversation to media matters. You do have a life outside the library media center. Participate in curriculum discussions, point out how library media services can contribute to curriculum planning and development.

- Stop in the faculty lounge and in teacher workrooms. Join in discussions where you can inject ways library media activities can be integrated into teaching plans. This is an important part of your job.

INVOLVE TEACHERS

- Ask teachers to help you decide what books to discard in their subject areas.

- Invite a teacher to work with you on a display case (e.g., display examples of students' line drawing along with books on drawing).

- Check to see how teachers in your building have used library media services in the last month or two. List the services each used. Use this profile to go after those teachers who seldom use library media services. Ask yourself—and them—why? See Figure 3–4 for an example of how to get them into the library.

- Survey the faculty from time to time. Develop a questionnaire (not too long) to find out what services they do and do not use, why, and their level of satisfaction. You seriously want to know answers to these and other questions, but write them with some humor. Use the responses to plan improvements in your services. Now I realize that the person who says you never let him know about media center services is the very same person whom you have seen discard, unread, these brilliant flyers you send out. So let your survey also be a way to inform these teachers of the services available.

- When you order new material, note the name of the teacher who will find it useful on the order card. Once the items have been processed, generate a personal list for each teacher to let her or him know about these new titles of specific interest. If you use multislip order forms, send one of the slips to the concerned teacher along with a note saying that these new titles are available and can be picked up in the media center, or that the teacher can return the slip to you and have the books delivered to his room or his mailbox (see

Figure 3–4 Instakwik Form

SOME OF YOU (and you know who you are, my dollings) have not yet visited the Library Media Center!! It couldn't be anything we've said or done that keeps you from our sides, because we haven't even had a chance to say or do *anything* to delight (or offend) you yet. It must be that you've been so busy that you haven't had time to come in for a chat, a browse, a snack, a photocopy, a preplanning session, or a book (not to mention a gossip).

SO WHY DON'T YOU:
Fill in the INSTAKWIK INFO FORM below and return it to the official Library Media Mailbox and *we* will send *YOU* absolutely FREE, something to make your job easier and/or your day brighter.

* *

INSTAKWIK INFO FORM

Name _____   Subject _____

Hobbies/Interests _____ Room _____

I'd like you to send me:

    ___Magazines   ___Books

    ___Book Reviews   ___Newspaper Article Reprints

    ___AV Materials   ___Magazine Article Reprints

    ___Computer Info   ___Other on the Following topics:

                                    _____

                                      _____

Drop this in the Library Media Mailbox or call Ext. 282 if you're in a big hurry. (You really should learn to relax more.)

Figures 3–5 and 3–6). You can include the same message on computer print-out lists. This system personalizes your new-titles list and avoids that long, dull list of all new titles, only some of which are of interest to any one teacher.

- Inform faculty of new book arrivals with the "Christmas Anytime" Project. When a large book order arrives, pull out the books purchased for a specific teacher, project, or subject area. Use Post-it notes to flag chapters, illustrations, or other details you know might be of particular interest. Divide the books into groups by subject area and individuals, and package them attractively. Put the biggest stacks into boxes that you wrap in shipping paper or newspaper and address them to the appropriate teacher with a colorful, hand-written label. Put some stacks into attractive paper shopping bags recycled from the local mall. Gift wrap and label the smallest stacks. Ask student assistants to deliver these "gifts" to teachers with notes explaining that these are new books they might find interesting. Ask the teachers to look over the books and then return them so that they can be shared with other teachers. The time spent in preparing the packages is more than repaid in the fun teachers have in opening their "gifts," and their "presents" are a topic of conversation at lunch. What good PR! The books are returned promptly and teachers appreciate this method of presentation. (Note: It's hard to believe, but there are still people who think that books come to schools selected by someone, perhaps at the state education department, perhaps at some book warehouse in the sky. How surprised they are when they learn that *we* select books for our curriculum and our students' needs.)

- Encourage English teachers to read young-adult (YA) books to familiarize themselves with the excellent titles in this category. Too many high school teachers limit their assignments to *Moby Dick*, *Great Expectations*, and other classics. Some of them think YA books are simple, poorly written, formula plots with little literary merit. Gather some YA classics and talk about them at an English department meeting, at an after-school session in the media center, or on a teachers' conference day. Let teachers know that there are quality YA novels that have great appeal to teen-age readers. (An entry for your Book of Golden Memories: A student who never read a book takes a book you press on him—*The Outsider*, perhaps—and the next day he comes to you and asks for another good book. It really happens, but we must get more teachers to give YA books a chance.)

- Create historical fiction bibliographies for social studies teachers. If your teachers have never used fiction with their classes, they will be surprised and pleased at how novels can bring a historical period or event to life for students. Hard to believe, but this is a totally new idea for some teachers.

Figure 3–5 New Book Announcement—1

NEW BOOKS in Beech South High School Library Media Center

When you come in, bring these slips with you.

If you can't come, call us at ext. 235 and we will put the books you want in your mail box.

Service is our motto, sort of.

hf
em

Figure 3–6 New Book Announcement—2

- Announce before the end of the school year that you plan to do a "How I Spent My Summer Vacation" showcase in the fall. Ask teachers, students, administrators, and others to bring in photos and brochures from their trips and display them along with books on water sports, national parks, families, and regions of the country. Give credit to your contributors.

- Plan a Pretty Baby Contest. Ask teachers to bring in pictures of themselves as infants or young children. Give each picture a number and post it in the display case. On a contest form, list the names of teachers who brought pictures and ask students to match up baby pictures and names. Award prizes to the winner and the runner-up. Seeing their teachers as youngsters reminds students that their teachers actually were children once.

- When teachers comment to you about lack of on-line services in the media center, the paucity of magazine subscriptions, the scarcity of up-to-date materials, ask them to go with you to the principal—not as punishment for complaining, but to let her know that the educational program is suffering because of the shortage of media center budget funds. You have certainly spoken of this before. It is often when teachers bring up this subject that notice is finally taken.

PROVIDE INFORMATION

- Be your school's source for information on local, state, and national officials—their addresses, phone numbers, and the names of their aides. Provide guidelines on how to write effective letters to legislators.

- Each year purchase teacher income-tax-preparation guides. You may find you need several copies.

- Announce the long-awaited arrival of annual volumes with a flyer or an announcement posted on the door to the media center. "The 1998 edition of *The World Almanac* has arrived."

- Become the headquarters for vacation planning. Put a student volunteer in charge of requesting free tourist kits from various states and foreign countries. Purchase travel books for the collection, and keep a file of hotel discount plans. Students will also find this information useful for some of their projects.

- Prepare briefly annotated bibliographies as teachers request them or as you see the need. Add new titles as new books and other materials are added to the collection. It is easy to up-date the list if you keep it in the computer. Keep print copies of the lists on hand for students who lose theirs or were absent the day they were distributed. Anticipating teachers' needs will win you gold stars from them.

- Periodically, print out a list of the bibliographies you have produced and send it to the teachers. Such a list also lets your building administrators know about the broad range of topics you are called on to cover in the library media center.

- Check through listings of upcoming cable television programs each month and let individual teachers know about programs you think will be of particular interest to them. Provide a tear-off they can return to you to request videotaping.

- Develop a strong working relationship with the in-service coordinator in your building. Offer to present a course on how teachers (and ultimately kids) can benefit from media center services, on new technologies in the media center, on how to develop new resource-based instruction units, or on some other aspect of teacher-library media cooperation.

- Keep a copy of the master schedule for your building in the media center. It is frequently important to know where a particular teacher is at any given time—not just for you but for others as well.

- Suggest that all the teachers in your school use the same bibliographic style. Enlist support from teachers who most often assign research projects. Be a part of the committee that gets input from all concerned teachers and develops the plan.

PROVIDE RECOGNITION

- Send notes congratulating teachers when appropriate, also get-well and sympathy cards and the like. You can create interesting, attractive cards with computer programs.

- In your report to administrators, mention the names of teachers who have been especially cooperative. Send copies to the cite-worthy teachers.

- Did you and a teacher develop an especially good resource-based instructional unit together? Let your professional association know about it and volunteer the two of you to present it at a conference.

- Pass on to teachers any positive comments you hear about them from students or other teachers. Everyone likes to hear good things about themselves. Forget the negative things you hear.

- Schedule a lunch-time or after-school series of programs featuring as speakers staff members in your building or district who have interesting and perhaps unusual hobbies or areas of expertise outside their professional jobs. This gives the staff members the chance to show off talents that are not widely known. Some of the new respect and prestige that flow to the speaker on these occasions will come to you, who not only learned of the heretofore hidden talents and experiences of these staff members but also served as their promoter. Lest you think that you have few if any such talented people in your school or district, consider the areas below and see if it reminds you of someone (or several someones).

Skills

— The elementary teacher whose interest in steam engines has led him to become an engineer on a steam railroad during summer vacations.

— The social studies teacher who is the captain of his own fishing boat on weekends and in the summer.

— The third-grade teacher who is a gourmet cook.

— The chemistry teacher who is a photographer and has presented one-man shows of his work.

— The social studies teacher who carves full-sized merry-go-round figures.

— The reading teacher who sings in a highly popular gospel quartet.

— The guidance counselor who plays in a chamber music group.

— The math teacher whose tennis talent has made him a world-ranked competitor in his age group.

— The chorus director who grows vegetables organically.

Collections and Crafts

— The auto-shop teacher who collects, rebuilds, and refurbishes vintage cars and rents them out for motion-picture shoots.

— The sixth-grade teacher who collects vintage clothing.

— The English teacher who creates such beautiful stained-glass designs that people commission her to make pieces for them.

— The principal who produces and directs plays for community theaters.

— The teacher who wins national awards for the decoys he carves.

— The teacher who creates in his wood-working shop at home museum-quality furniture reproductions.

—The librarian who stitches quilts that are works of art.

— The driver-education teacher who creates delicate, stunningly beautiful Christmas ornaments with beads, lace, crystals, and ribbons.

Travel and Other Experiences

— The teachers who serve in National Guard or Reserve units and are called to active duty in national emergencies.

— The middle-school teacher who is elected to the board of education in the district where he lives.

— The social studies teacher who ran in and finished both the Boston and New York Marathons.

— The teacher who, while on sabbatical, worked as an aide to the county executive.

— The physical education teacher who is a rock climber.

— The librarian who has trekked in the Himalayas.

— The studio art teacher who travels the world in the summer with a camera and a clean shirt.

Other Interests

— The custodian who is a published short-story author.

— The business teacher who prepares income-tax returns as a sideline.

— The librarian who is a dedicated operagoer and knows more about opera than anyone else you know.

— The middle-school teacher who has become an authority on the Underground Railroad.

— The principal who is a beekeeper.

FACULTY READING

• Prepare a reading list for faculty members of titles they will enjoy. Everybody needs to get away from the stuff they feel they are required to read. Teachers may use their public libraries for this and other services included on this list, but they are in your building every day and you want to bring them into your library.

• Encourage faculty and other staff to visit the media center before long holidays and summer vacation to check out all the books they haven't had time to read during the year (see Figure 3–7). Have a supply of boxes or heavy paper bags to carry away their finds.

• Send teachers copies of reviews of books they may find interesting.

• Buy some adult fiction, including titles from bestseller lists. High-school students as well as teachers will use these purchases.

• In an elementary or middle school, start a collection of adult bestsellers. Ask interested teachers to contribute the cost of one book and to collaborate on selecting titles. Keep these books in the back room or someplace out of bounds to students. Let teachers know that only members of the contributing group may borrow these books.

Figure 3–7 Summer Reading

Come by the Library on Thursday or Friday next week and check out your books for SUMMER READING. We have boxes and shopping bags—or bring your own.

Don't plan to read? Drop by and say "Au revoir."

KEEPING UP

- Keep current on copyright laws. Post copyright information on the photo-copiers in your building. At least once a year send out to teachers an up-to-date flyer about copyright rules.

- Let teachers in the social studies and other departments know that you would like to attend their professional association conferences so you can come up to speed on new methods, materials, ideas in their subject areas.

- Develop a plan with your principal for taking a team of teachers and administrators to a library conference that promises to have some particularly good programs on how media specialists and teachers can work together to improve kids' learning.

- Set up some afternoon sessions to familiarize teachers with some of the new technologies in the library media center. They need to know how to access information themselves and how they can incorporate it into their assignments. You may want to try this either on a facultywide basis or work at it by departments.

SPECIAL COLLECTIONS AND SERVICES

- Maintain poster- and art-print collections, and make an attractive listing that you give teachers. Let them know they can borrow these materials for their rooms. If you laminate the posters and prints, they will suffer less wear and tear, but don't expect miracles.

- Inform teachers that you maintain a file of courses offered at local colleges, continuing education opportunities, and other such information. Remind them that you have access to ERIC and other information sources they need.

- If you are working during the summer, volunteer to water teachers' plants if they bring them to the media center and take them back in the fall.

- Some teachers may be able to use the magazines you discard. Let them know when throw-away time comes.

- Volunteer to let students do make-up tests in the library media center.

- Give a student volunteer the responsibility of clipping and filing manufacturers' cents-off coupons. Invite teachers and other staff members to select the ones they want.

- Let teachers leave materials to be photocopied and picked up later. Do not include tests in this offer, because security can be a problem. Put a volunteer in charge of the service.

- Make available mail-order catalogues. Put a student in charge of weeding out dated issues.

- Offer to send copies of the table of contents from journals and periodicals to faculty members. Find out from them what publications they want to hear about.

- Make space in the media center workroom for the laminator, the transparency maker, and the photocopier. Keep write-on film and pens on hand.

DEPARTMENTAL INTERACTION

- Work up some ideas on how you can attract teachers, especially from departments that don't usually schedule classes or use library media services. Develop in broad outline some research-based teaching units on topics you know teachers cover. Once a teacher agrees to use your ideas, work with him to flesh out details. Anticipate ways to cooperate with teachers—don't wait to be called upon. The first seven ideas listed below are projects a middle-school librarian, Ellen Ballin, conceived to attract teachers in departments some of which did not often use the library:

— Foreign language: Plan a culture fair. Each student researches a country and develops a travel brochure containing information about life in that country. Include in the unit communicating with students in that country via the Internet.

— Mathematics: When students are studying decimals, develop a Dewey Decimal Derby contest. Relate the Dewey Decimal System to their class assignments. Assign Dewey numbers to students and have them arrange themselves in call-number order. This project reinforces the idea that concepts learned in class are useful in other classes and other circumstances.

— Art: Have students select a state and locate information about it that will aid them in designing a state logo using the state flower, the state bird, geographical features, and other information.

— Music: Ask students to research instruments of the orchestra, their designs, sounds, place in the orchestra, and music written especially for them.

— Technology: Have the class develop a huge time-line mural based on famous inventors, their inventions, and how the inventions have benefited mankind. Use a roll of sturdy paper and mount it on the wall around the room.

— Social studies: For a project on voting, assign high- or middle-school students issues to research and bring together in a book for the third grade. When the book is completed, the students visit the elementary school to talk about the importance of voting in American life. A copy of the book is left for the elementary school library and one is added to the secondary school's library collection.

— Careers: Each student selects a career to research. It may be one that the student thinks she would like to pursue or one that just sounds interesting. Interview someone who does that kind of work. Discover what the career entails and the training and preparation it requires. What high-school courses would be useful to someone entering the field?

— English: Produce a class newspaper including articles on school events, music and book reviews, sports, social issues, weather, cartoons, editorials, and so on. This project involves reading newspapers to become familiar with what they contain and with different writing styles. Students use newspapers, books, on-line services, and other library materials.

— Woodworking shop: For a birdhouse project, ask students to research the birds of the area and learn why different birds need different types of houses. Locate and select appropriate building plans. Figure how much material will be needed to construct the birdhouse.

— Singles survival: Each student will prepare a week's food budget using newspaper advertisements to learn about best buys, sales, and money-saving coupons. This assignment calls for researching healthful foods and meal planning, and includes learning how to read labels on packaging for nutritional information.

— Physical education: Students will locate in books, videos, and magazines exercises for developing muscles in different areas of the body. Each prepares a handout to distribute to the class and teaches the class how to do the exercise.

— Earth science: Students collect and identify various kinds of local rocks. They research what geologic forces created them, how old they might be, and the practical uses of the rocks (for buildings, gravel, walkways, statues, fences, fireplaces, polishing jewelry, etc.).

— Language skills: The *All About You Project* requires students first to research the meaning of their first names and other forms that their names might take in other languages (e.g., John, Jean, Giovanni; Catherine, Karen, Katrina). They then find out the most-often used girls' and boys' names and which family names are the most common in the United States. Next, it's time to learn family history or family stories from an older family member. (In selecting this assignment be sensitive to children in the class who may not live with or have access to family members who know even a small bit of family history.) Then locate a newspaper published on the day the student was born or an issue of *Time* or *Newsweek* from that week to learn what was going on in the country, city, region, and world. What movies were playing? Who was president? What famous people share the same birthday with the student? Ask students what name they would choose if they could change their names. Be aware of names that parents create for their children; those students may want to find out how such names came to be.

— Economics: Investment game. This is a long-term game, stretching over the bulk of the year. "Give" each student in class $500 to invest in the stock market. Using stock-market information in newspapers, magazines, and on-line services, the students decide which stocks to "purchase" and when and whether to "sell." They will need to check the market quotations regularly to keep track of their investments, as well as maintain careful records of their investments. At the end of the game determine who made the most successful investments. It isn't always the teacher!

- Develop a strong working relationship with at least one teacher in each department. Spend extra time in joint planning on instructional units with that teacher. Ask the teacher to report good results in department meetings. When other teachers in the department see how students benefit, perhaps they too will want to work more closely with you.

- Become knowledgeable about competency-test results in your building. Work with teachers to develop ways to counter poor scores on certain items.

- Suggest to art teachers a design unit in which students create covers for books they have read. Put the covers into plastic see-through jackets and leave them on the books to dress up the collection. The student's name should, of course, be on the cover as the designer.

- Know your teachers and their courses so well that you can go to them with suggestions for ways you can work with them on particular units of study. Don't wait for them to come to you.

School Nurse

Send the school nurse copies of articles she may find interesting. Let her know about computer on-line resources and new books dealing with health topics. Other ways you and the school nurse can work together include:

— Work together on a program for parents about nutrition, common health problems of youngsters, physical checkups, and services the health office makes available to students. Prepare for distribution Read-More-About-It lists of library resources on these topics.

— Make available in the library brochures from the health office, and place library brochures on health topics in the health office.

— Ask the school nurse to keep you up-to-date on newly developing or potential health problems in the school. Share with her your observations of possible student health problems.

— Be sure to keep handy information from the school nurse on how to deal with such emergencies as epileptic seizures, choking, falls, cuts, and other injuries. You and your staff must be able to deal with such emergencies until the nurse arrives on the scene.

— Report to the school nurse any evidence you have that a child is a victim of abuse. In your district, regulations may require that this information be reported directly to the principal. Be aware of the steps you should take.

Guidance Counselors

Work with the guidance counselors to amass a stellar collection on careers. Some books may be in the guidance department collection, others in the media center collection, and some should be in both places. Make sure that each department knows what the other has, and apprise each other of recently published materials and additions to the collections. Some other areas in which you can cooperate with the guidance department include:

PARENT INFORMATION

— Working with counselsors, plan programs for parents on financial aid for their college-bound youngsters. Put together a display of books and computer software on financial aid, talk about the availability and use of these information sources, and produce bibliographies for them.

— Take part in programs on how to select a college. Inform parents and students of the books and computer software in the media center collection on choosing a college.

DISPLAYS AND OTHER INFORMATION

— Set aside display space in the library for materials on military service careers.

— Make sure that students know about and have access to information about jobs, local and regional employment advertisements, and books (and other information) on writing resumes and preparing for job interviews. Make up short bibliographies on these topics and copy articles from newspapers and magazines.

— Maintain a file on student volunteer opportunities in the community.

— Keep road maps on hand of the county and perhaps of a broader area so you can help students find their way to job opportunities. Don't express surprise when students don't know how to get to a nearby town; many families never take their youngsters anywhere.

— Have available in the library flyers and other materials produced by the guidance department about mental health, teenage pregnancies, alcoholism, child abuse, and other counseling topics.

— Create bibliographies of teenage fiction on such topics as family problems, teen pregnancy, alcoholism, and teenagers with physical and mental handicaps. Youngsters can learn about themselves and others from excellent works of fiction written for their age level.

COLLEGE AND CAREER DAYS

— Along with the guidance department and other staff, organize a Career Day in your school. Invite people from your community and elsewhere to come into the library to talk about their jobs. This could be an all-day program featuring concurrent sessions from which students select those they want to attend.

— Be a part of College Day activities, when representatives from various colleges talk to students and distribute information. Display books and computer programs on college selection in the library.

INFORMATION TO COUNSELORS

— Send counselors reviews on material they might be interested in.

— Share with counselors information on careers, not forgetting those students who may not be planning to continue their education after high school.

— Ask the guidance counseling center to set out bibliographies on various topics of materials and information sources available in the library.

SCHOOL SUPPORT STAFF

Secretaries, custodians, aides, cafeteria workers, maintenance staff, and other building support staff all significantly influence the job we do and the image of the library media center. Most of these people are residents of the community (there may even be a requirement that they live in the district). They are parents of our students, and they probably vote in school district elections for board members and the budget. It is important that we have their good will and their support. They are in unique positions that give them insight into what goes on in the school, and are conduits for information to the community. Custodians and other support staff in the schools can be valuable public relations agents for the library media programs in the community.

Custodians tend to be an overworked, underappreciated group who are vital to the well-being of a school. Without them, our environment would be plagued by filth, overflowing wastebaskets, burned-out light bulbs, and windows so grubby that the sun can't come through. We call the custodians to assemble and put up new shelving without delay. They deliver book orders left at the delivery entrance. We may need them to shift furniture for the weekly meeting. We shriek for them when a mouse problem materializes. When the ballast in the lighting goes, or the U-joint under the sink in the workroom gives up, we need them *fast*. True, the library media center may not be very high on their list of priorities, certainly not up there with the principal's office. But if we want the media center to be clean and in good repair, we need to get the custodial staff on our side—although we may never rank as high as the principal.

Secretaries in the district office, the front office, or elsewhere in our buildings are in positions where they can complicate our lives or make things easier for us. On the negative side, they can make it difficult for us to get an appointment with an administrator, "lose" some of our budget pages, fail to pass on our messages, or delay sending administrators' messages to us. On the positive side, they can shield us from the salespeople who appear without appointments, remind us of budget-spending deadlines, or perhaps whisper in our ears that there is some surplus money we can request from the principal for an item we very much need but can't afford. Secretaries seem to know everything that goes on in the district and the building, and how nice it is to be one of the people with whom they like to share information.

It isn't difficult to list ways other building support staff are helpful to us. Part of our job is getting to know them, to make them aware that we appreciate them and what they do for us. Too often, we behave as though building support staff are invisible; we concentrate too little attention on those hard-working people who deserve our understanding and respect.

Consider some of these ways to help win friends for the library media center from the school's support staff.

LIBRARY MEDIA SERVICES

- Find out from secretaries, aides, and custodians what magazines they would like to have routed to them. Put a student volunteer in charge of preparing the routing form when the issue comes off the magazine rack. Make sure everyone understands the time limits you have set and sends the magazine on to the next person on the list promptly.

- Let school support staff know when you have new books that you think they will like. This means you must know the individuals and their interests.

- Let members of the support staff know when you have discarded materials to give away.

- Offer to make copies of home-produced videos and audiotapes for support staff. This is a job your trained student volunteers can do. Offer to laminate materials for them.

SHOW APPRECIATION

- At Christmas have gifts for school support staff: a box of candy or home-made cookies for the custodians' lounge; something for the secretaries in the front office; and something for the teachers' aides with whom you come in contact. Don't forget the cafeteria workers who provided refreshments for a meeting on very short notice. Include support staff on your distribution list for Christmas or other holiday greetings.

- On Secretaries' Day, send greeting cards to the secretaries in your building and the district office, thanking them for the ways they have helped you.

- During National Education Week, plan an appreciation party after school in the media center to honor the aides in your building (see Figure 3–8). Ask the principal to speak about how aides contribute to the education of young-sters.

- Send thank-you notes when a custodian has been particularly helpful. Send copies to the principal for the custodian's personnel file.

- Create a form you can send to the custodial or maintenance staff when you have a problem you want them to deal with. Indicate the problem, the date, and the degree of urgency. Keep a copy for your file. Be sure to date when you send it and when it is acted upon. (This is not as ominous as it sounds.) The custodians may adopt your form for use throughout the building. Using this information, you can let administrators know when maintenance and custodial staffs members have performed their jobs in the library in an especially praiseworthy manner.

Figure 3–8 Thank You Party

To a special Thank You Party

for: Our faithful library helpers

on: Friday, June 13th

where: Library workroom

time: During your lunch
      period

Chapter 4

BUILDING ADMINISTRATORS: TAKE ME TO YOUR LEADERS

THE PRINCIPAL

In the "olden days," all principals learned to say, "The library is the heart of the school." In those bad old days, many of us believed that the sentence carried in it nearly everything that the principal knew about libraries. We must hasten to add, however, that this did not mean that administrators had hardened their hearts against library media programs, their functions and requirements, but in all likelihood simply reflected their noncognition of the central role the library plays in the academic achievement of students and in accomplishing the mission of the school.

Fortunately, in most places times have changed, and so have many principals and other building administrators. Schools of education do not seem, however, to be the source of their increased knowledge about library media programs. It is more than likely that library media specialists have "educated" their administrators to the multifaceted role of media centers in youngsters' education, or that the administrators have worked in buildings with excellent library media programs. What a joy to get a new building administrator and discover that she is already a strong supporter of the media center! But should a new administrator come in who is not knowledgeable about what we do and how it impacts the entire learning program, we know that we have the task of making sure she gets the library media message. Such people may believe that they know the whole story, but this is often not the case, and you must build from where they are.

You and your administrator are partners in the education endeavor. You are on the same side, working toward the same goals, with the same needs for support and loyalty. The requirements of your job closely parallel those of your principal: you are called on to administer the library media program; the principal oversees the entire school. This similarity in roles places you in a position where you can get to know the principal better and can develop a closer working relationship than can the average classroom teacher. Use your advantage to strengthen the principal's support for the library media program.

THE PRINCIPAL AS DECISION MAKER

Principals have an enormous amount of authority over library media programs, in some districts, even deciding whether to have a library media specialist on the school's staff. When a principal in the district elects to have no media specialist in his building, the media specialists in the district can join forces to let that principal know how students benefit educationally with professional media center staffing, as well as how drastically they are disadvantaged without a media specialist. Parent advocates can be enlisted, too. Perhaps a new principal will never fully understand the educational advantages but will "go along" because peers advocate it. A true program of resource-based use and learning cannot exist without a certified library media specialist to develop and implement a program. That some states require a library in every school but do not require a library media specialist to put these resources to work demonstrates that we advocates of library services for children have much to accomplish with our PR efforts!

Principals also have the final word in some districts over how the media center will be funded for materials, equipment, and support staff. In the ongoing competition for building-budget dollars, the pressure from all departments is intense. We must be able to justify our budget requests using all the persuasive powers we have to maintain services to students and to acquire the resources needed to support particular curriculum projects. We must learn how to exert, skillfully, appropriate influence for the library needs of our students.

How do we persuade the principal that the library media center program needs additional funding for more materials, space, staff? It isn't enough to say that libraries are important, because we, and the principal, too, know they are. Building administrators need facts. They want to see results they can use to obtain funds. They must operate on their building allocations, or they must seek additional funds from the district. They rely upon you to develop some measures of superior performance by students who make full use of the library media services.

PROVIDE INFORMATION FOR DECISIONS

Principals want to know how additional funding would improve the educational achievement of kids. What specific needs will be met by additional materials? How will having more staff impact on education in the building? It may be true that additional support staff will lighten your load, but that is not a legitimate reason for the request. You might say that an aide would take over clerical tasks, freeing you to spend more time working directly with students and teachers. What educational purpose would more space serve? Principals want to know specifics that only you can provide. All your requests must be justified in terms of how they would benefit teachers, administrators, and, most importantly, students.

Before you go to your meeting with the principal, get support from department chairs, grade-level chairs, and individual teachers who know exactly how students would benefit from your plans.

Present your clearly thought-out proposals to the principal in an organized manner, and be very specific in your justifications. Give the principal an outline showing what you need, why you need it, and how much you think it will cost. Beware of using round numbers; they're deadly. Principals and all administrators will merely conclude you're guessing at costs, which, actually, you may be.

Present your principal with such powerful data that he will recognize the need to take funding from some other project, if necessary, and add it to your budget. For this to happen, he must believe in the strong link between a quality media program and student achievement. So be prepared: Be specific about the benefits that will flow to students from his funding of your request. Be willing to develop more statistics, documentation, and hard facts if he needs them. If he plans to go to the district for increased building funds, he must have as much compelling information as you can give him.

We cannot afford to be modest, shy, retiring, or reticent about how our programs are involved with all departments of the school, all grade levels, all the teachers in the school, and all the students. We are an integral part of the teaching team and of the instructional program in the school. We are not a support service, an add-on, a nice-to-have frill. By keeping the principal and other building administrators fully informed about media center matters, we can ensure that no one thinks that, because we are not in a classroom setting or actually holding forth before a class of youngsters at the moment, we have nothing to do and can take a study hall for an absent teacher.

The principal's perception of the library media program influences that of everyone else in the building. Perhaps the most crucial task we have is to ensure that the principal not only acknowledges that the library media program is central in accomplishing the mission of the school but that he also fully supports the program in the building and is its vocal advocate at the district level.

DEPARTMENT CHAIRPERSONS

We want department chairs to understand what media center services contribute to students and teachers in their departments. The chairs are in positions to urge reluctant teachers to consult with us on planning instructional units, to become aware of the broad array of materials in the collection, and to use the technology with which they may not yet be familiar. We look to department chairs to support us as we work to keep up with the new materials, new technologies, and staffing. Once they understand how library media support the instruction in their departments, they will join us in supporting our budget requests.

This symbiosis comes into play when, from time to time, department chairs come to us seeking our support for their budget requests. It is in the best interest of students, departments, and the media center when we can cooperate with others to help them achieve their goals. Perhaps we can share the cost of a project that a department wants to undertake if we, for example, negotiate housing the project's materials and equipment in the media center—where it will be useful to students in all departments.

We should expect all building administrators to speak out for the library media program as district budgets are being formulated. A district media coordinator will participate in district budget planning, but in the absence of a coordinator (which is the sad situation in many districts) there may be no one other than the building administrators to serve as advocates for library media services for the district's children. If we have supplied administrators with our plans, statistics, and projected costs, they will have the right information to use in presenting our case to the district budget planners.

The library media program must always be visible. We must be zealous in our efforts to ensure that it is never forgotten or allowed to slip the administrator's mind. Below are some ways to keep administrators informed about and aware of the library media program.

ACTIVITIES

CEREMONIES AND CELEBRATIONS

- Plan a ribbon-cutting ceremony for some new service in your media center. Invite the principal to cut the ribbon. This is a good photo opportunity.

- Invite the principal, assistant principal, and department chairs to read aloud in the media center.

- Nominate a supportive building administrator for a "Building Administrator of the Year Award" given by your state library media association. If your organization does not have such an award begin a campaign to establish one.

- Write a welcoming letter to the new principal, assistant principal, or department chair.

- Commemorate the date the principal joined the staff with a message that notes some highlights of his or her time in the position.

- Ask administrators to participate in library read-ins.

- Take your principal to breakfast during School Library Media Month. Ask other media specialists to invite their principals. Make a big thing of it. This is a natural photo opportunity and a suitable occasion for a district newsletter article.

- With other media specialists in your district, consider establishing an annual Building Administrator Award. In a large district you may limit nominations to principals. In a small district, you might include principals, assistant principals, department chairs, and grade-level chairs in order to make the pool larger. Develop criteria for the award so the selection is not made purely subjectively. Present the award at a board of education meeting, making sure the proclamation includes specifically how the recipient supported the library media program in her building.

MEETINGS, ETC.

- Invite each department chair to hold a department meeting in the media center (see Figure 4–1). Ask for a few minutes on the agenda to show them new items (already on display) that will be especially useful to that department.

- Attend as many subject department meetings as you can. Ask for time to speak about media center services, materials, and your availability for planning resource-based instructional units.

- Administrators may have some grounds for thinking that all media specialists are greedy, complaining, and fussy, because it may seem that is all they hear from us. The cure? Plan a "Surprise the Principal Day": Meet with her and—here's the surprise—don't complain about anything, but do thank her for her support and encouragement. Do not report this to the school newspaper. She may want to, however.

- Invite the principal to hold a faculty meeting occasionally in the library media center.

- Request that the principal hold the orientation for new staff in the library media center. Arrange for a spot on her schedule.

- Schedule regular meetings with the principal to discuss media center matters. Prepare an agenda so you don't wander from topic to topic, but be ready to depart from it if the principal leads the way.

- Call your principal with some good news. Thank him for his support in making it happen.

Figure 4–1 Department Meetings

To:

From: Flowers and Mulcahy

Re: An Invitation

Date: October 1, 19—

You recognize this, we are sure, as our much-sought-after annual invitation to schedule one of your department meetings in the library. We want some time on your agenda to discuss common concerns, and we have some new things you and your teachers should know about.

Our coffee, tea, and cookie supplies have been replenished, our schedule book is open, and we await your call or visit to schedule a date. Do let us hear from you soon.

PLANNING

- Suggest to your principal that you be given planning time during school hours to work cooperatively with teachers.

- Be sure that department chairs urge their teachers to make full use of media center services and resources in their lesson plans. Some teachers may feel threatened, fearing that this will mean more work for them, so emphasize your willingness to support, share, and team with them, and how by working together you can lighten their load and make their results more satisfying.

- Become a creative budget developer. Design a request for funding around an instructional need (e.g., a new social studies requirement from the state education department), and include all the components you see as necessary. Involve the department chair in planning, but if some materials and equipment can be used by other departments, specify that. For really big projects, consider phasing in the purchases over several years.

- Maintain a list of materials you would purchase if your principal told you there was extra money that had to be spent by tomorrow. Sometimes dreams do come true.

SHARING INFORMATION

- Contact the department of educational administration at a university near you (you may have taken courses there) and volunteer to do a presentation on the role of the library media center program to a class of future administrators. You could do this yourself, or your local library media association may want to undertake this as a project. Too many administrators come into their positions knowing very little about what goes on in the media center or how vital it is to back it.

- Specify to administrators how much books, periodicals, and other materials cost, and how many titles your budget allotment will allow for. Will your budget buy one new book per student this year? One book per three students? A goal of one book per student is not outrageous, so if you can do that already, then up your ratio.

- Save some of the weeded outdated books to show administrators and board members when you request increased funds for books. Use the really "destructive" ones, such as the old favorites that project that "Someday, Man Will Walk on the Moon" or that promote the glories of asbestos as a building material.

- Demonstrate in a dramatic way the increased cost of materials and how few books the book budget can really buy:

— Load on a book truck all the new books purchased with the year's budget. Photograph the truck, front and back, and use the photos on a flyer with the caption, "The above pictures represent $ XXXX worth of new library books. They don't even fill one book truck."

— On the bottom half of the flyer use figures published annually in *School Library Journal* that show average book prices for children's and young adult books and for other categories of books over a period of several years.

— Send copies of the flyer to other media specialists in the district to use in their budget preparations. Post copies and leave them up on Open House Night for parents to see and leaves them up for several weeks so students, faculty, and administrators become aware of how many books the budget can buy. Flyers arouse comments about how few books the budget allotment adds to the collection.

• Send administrators copies of all the printed materials you distribute.

• Send administrators carefully selected reprints of newspaper and periodical articles you think may interest them. They need not be about libraries per se, but about child/youth development and social or economic issues to which you may link library media services.

• Send administrators copies of your goals and objectives for the year, even if they don't require them.

• Prepare and send short, snappy reports frequently (see chapter 8).

• Ask the principal to include the library on tours given to visitors.

• Remind administrators of interlibrary loan services, for their own as well as school needs.

• Distribute occasionally a "Did You Know?" flyer to both building and district administrators in which you list a variety of little-known statistics about the media center. You may want to include the number of bibliographies you prepared last month (last week, last six weeks) and the broad array of topics covered; how many students came to the library during a certain number of school days and the average per day; circulation over a period of time figured in average number of books per student in school; the average number of students per square feet of floor space on a particularly busy day. This last figure means absolutely nothing, but usually draws a smile from your readers. Of course, it may show that you need more space.

• Think of all the things you can count: number of cups of coffee you poured for your coffee breaks over a period of time and how many you actually consumed; how many times *Sports Illustrated* (or some other popular magazine) circulated or was requested; the shortest time a popular periodical remained in the library media center before it was ripped off. Since you really don't have time to count all of these things, you are allowed to estimate. Board of education members and the faculty may enjoy receiving this occasional publication. Use a clever graphic and photocopy on brightly colored paper. Vary your statistics with each issue, and keep it short, snappy, and light. Being zany occasionally counts in your favor, as do flexibility, friendliness, and fairness.

VISITS

- Arrange for a building administrator to join you in visiting a nearby district that has an outstanding library media program, or one that does well something that you want to do. If it has something to do with computers or some other equipment, so much the better.

- Your job is to know what is going on in nearby school districts, and, even more important, how to get your administrators to buy into a good initiative. The word "lobbying" may come to mind, but skillfully persuading your administrator to your way of thinking is part of your mission; you are the advocate for the best possible media center program for the kids in your school.

- Invite a building administrator to attend a library conference or workshop with you to become better informed or up-dated on library media matters. Be sure that you visit together the exhibits to see new products. Be prepared to talk about your plans for new services as you look at exhibits.

BE A VOLUNTEER

- Volunteer for the committee selecting and/or interviewing a new principal or department chair. This is a good way to get someone in the job who is supportive of the role of the media center. Call the media specialist in the school or district where a candidate now works to learn how this person supports the library media program. This is "checking references."

- Write an article on library media centers for the principal's local, regional, or state professional organization's journal. Volunteer to present a program at an organization's annual conference. Administrators often know less about the educational function of the library media center than about any other department in the school, and the journals that they read seldom contain articles about the role of libraries. You have an opportunity to fill this educational void.

- Volunteer to serve on building committees—not just any committee, but those that deal with substantive educational matters. Your goal is to ensure that library media services are not omitted in planning for curriculum or other changes in the building. Serving as a chair of a highly visible committee puts you in a position to have some control over outcomes. Be vigilant in seeing to it that library media services are never lumped in with "school support services" but rather classed with the instructional services and programs where they belong.

- Volunteer library media center support on some project the administrators are undertaking.

- Route certain periodicals to administrators. (Control this carefully, or all the *Sports Illustrated* or *Muscle and Fitness* issues will end up in somebody's office.) Sending copies of table-of-contents pages may work better for you.

- Let administrators know that you are maintaining a file of materials from newspapers about your school. If you have inherited a file from your predecessor, it may be time to take steps to preserve old, crumbling papers, which can be commercially microfilmed at very little cost. Give a copy of the microfilm to the public library to be placed in their local-history collection. Include special editions about the history of your town.

- Gather a complete collection of your high school's yearbooks. Ask the yearbook sponsor to donate a copy each year, and let the community know you are seeking donations of copies from earlier years that may be missing. Become the source for the history of your school. Develop a security plan for student use of the yearbooks (they may not be able to resist the temptation to tear out a picture of Aunt Mabel when she was a senior—or of teachers when they joined the faculty thirty years ago).

- Offer to your principal such media center services as making transparencies for his presentations to parents, district administrators, the faculty, and conferences.

- Consider becoming a building or district administrator. You know the power and influence administrators have over programs in their buildings and districts. In such a position you could do much to strengthen library media programs.

FRIENDLY GESTURES

- When you receive compliments for media center services, share credit with your principal who gave you her support.

- Send post cards to your building administrators when you are on vacation or attending a conference. They should know you well enough by now to know that you are not currying favor but emphasizing collegial friendliness and courtesy.

- Send notes to building administrators about students who have performed well as student volunteers, have done some special service for the media center, or have in some way improved their behavior in the library media center.

- Invite the principal to drop in any time he's passing by.

- Send copies of cartoons on applicable topics.

- Send administrators notes about good teaching you have seen take place involving the media center and its materials.

Chapter 5

DISTRICT ADMINISTRATORS AND THE BOARD OF EDUCATION: FRIENDS IN HIGH PLACES

DISTRICT ADMINISTRATORS

Some of us work in districts where we seldom come in contact with the administrators in the district office. This is unfortunate, because these people make decisions that impact heavily on our professional lives. You should know them, and they should know you, your name, and the school you work in. You should know what their responsibilities are and how they relate to yours. You see, almost every administrator at the district level has some responsibility that bears on the library media program. Whatever the administrative organization in your district, find out who in the district office deals with curriculum, personnel, educational technology, pupil personnel services, and so forth.

Let's say your own building administrators do not support your efforts to increase funding for new materials for a statewide curriculum change. You may be able to convince, for example, the district curriculum director that the library media centers throughout the district should be funded to assist in this initiative. Or maybe your principal wants to but cannot fund a new support position for the library media staff. By joining with other media specialists, you may be able to influence a district-level decision to add staff to all library media centers.

Granted, getting to know district administrators and being known by them is difficult in a large urban district—but it's not impossible. It is not at all hard to do in a small setting, where you are one of a relatively small group of library media specialists—unlike English teachers or fourth-grade teachers, of whom there are many more.

You want central office administrators to know how kids benefit from excellent, well-supported, well-staffed, library media programs. They must be kept informed of how the library media program fosters the learning process and what it accomplishes in furthering the educational goals of the district. In school districts that have library media coordinators, that voice at the district level speaks for us, but having a coordinator in no way eliminates the need for each of us to communicate regularly and directly with the district office.

MEDIA SPECIALISTS COOPERATE

Especially in districts where there is no coordinator, the library media specialists in the district should unite, discuss common problems (and solutions), and plan strategies to communicate the library media message to the district level. Having a strong library media group or council does not, however, mean that the individual media specialist can relax his own efforts in maintaining contact with the district office administrators.

It should be evident that a media specialist in one school should not suggest that his program be supported more heavily than that of another school. If indeed there is a good reason that this might be the case, however, it should be thrashed out in the district library media group. Media specialists can work together to press for a fairer distribution of library media budget funds among schools. Principals can help here, too, by reinforcing that all of us together are pressing not for ourselves but for the benefit of the students.

PREVENT LIBRARY CUTS

In times when school systems are searching for ways to downsize staff in order to lower taxes, library media programs are too often targets for cuts. The mistaken idea seems to be that one media specialist can serve two or three buildings, leaving aides to "cover" when the media specialist is not there. This tactic does not take into account that kids need consistently professional, in-depth library services. They need easy access to their library media centers, and they should find certified library media specialists there to help fill the particular information needs of those students. Youngsters who do not attend schools with full-time certified library media specialists are being short-changed in their current education and are not being fully prepared for lifelong, independent learning.

The purpose of the library media program must be perfectly clear to those who make decisions that affect its well-being. It is the job of the library media specialist to guarantee that the message is sent, that it is received, that it is listened to, and that it is understood.

Warning: In some school districts there are restrictions on communicating directly with district administrators. Regulations may require that you follow a chain of command, that is, send your message to your principal, who then decides about sending it up to the district office. Check with your district policy handbook about the procedure to follow and do not go over your administrator's head. This practice can create enormous problems for you and damage your ability to influence administrators.

Some ways we can get our message to district administrators are listed here.

Offer Media Services

- Let district office administrators know that you can do interlibrary loans for them.

- Develop and send a flyer listing the many services that central office administrators can call on from your media center. Put some careful thought into this list; tuck in a few humorous items.

Send Invitations

- Ask central office administrators to attend and participate in media center Read-a-Thons.

- Invite the superintendent and assistant superintendents to come to the media center to observe some special event, to present an award or prize, or just to see what goes on. Be sure that something *is* going on.

Communicate

- Invite the superintendent to a meeting of all the library media specialists in the district on a date she chooses. Ask her to make some comments, but have an agenda containing items of concern to the media specialists. This must not degenerate into a gripe session! Have some handouts for her to take away. Everything must be oriented toward student achievement and the role the media specialist plays as teacher, information specialist, and instructional consultant.

- Inform the superintendent and the principal when you have been selected to serve on a committee or elected to an office in your local, state, or national professional organization. Let them know that your participation is good publicity for your district and your school.

- Write a note to the superintendent or other central office administrator congratulating him on being elected to an office in the state educational administrators' association.

- Be sure that your school district actively participates in your regional library system. Remind central office administrators of the advantages of system membership and participation. Ask the superintendent to designate a media specialist to be the official representative from your district to the system. The delegate should get release time to attend meetings and should share all information with other media specialists, the district office, and building principals. Volunteer to be the representative from your district.

Volunteer

- Volunteer to serve on highly visible building and district committees of administrators, teachers, and community members. If you can be appointed committee chairperson, so much the better. Service on a committee offers you the opportunity to take on a role that displays your expertise as an educator and leader outside the library setting.

- Find out who in the district office deals with important visitors to the district and ask that your library, a place where learning goes on, be included on visitors' tours.

- Ask to be appointed to the district public relations advisory committee. Be sure the library media centers in the district are included in all appropriate district public relations releases.

- If there is no written job description for library media specialists in your district, join with other media specialists to formulate one. Emphasize your roles as information specialist, teacher, and instructional consultant and the ways in which your job interacts with but differs dramatically from that of the classroom teacher. Include how your job affects student and teacher success, the public relations aspects of your position, your involvement in staff development, and how you collaborate and plan with teachers. If there is a job description, examine and revise it in light of how the requirements of your job have changed. Get approval of district administrators and the board of education for inclusion in the district policy handbook.

Recognize Supportive Administrators

- Take a thoughtful look at your administrators and nominate the one who has given greater-than-average support to library media programs for the Outstanding District Administrator award presented each year by your state professional association. If you can't in all good conscience recommend one, tell your administrators that such an award exists and what specific support was given by the administrator who won. If your administrator wins, give lots of attention to the award through the local newspapers, radio, and TV. Encourage all the media specialists in the district to attend the dinner at the conference when the award is presented. Back home in the district, arrange for a re-enactment of the award presentation at a board of education meeting. You'll be glad you took the time to do the paper work. Having an award winner is great PR for the district as well as for the library media program. It doesn't hurt your image any, either, to have been the person to nominate your administrator.

- If announced budget cuts did not materialize, staff positions were not cut, or funds earmarked for grass seed got added instead to the library media budget, then write thank-you letters to members of the district administration. Be grateful for even small victories.

- If to your deep regret, some or all of the tragic events listed above did come to pass, then write district administrators a letter expressing your sorrow and your recognition of the hard budget decisions they had to make. It is all right to let them know of your disappointment and how you must now make difficult decisions about cutting the library media program in such a way as to cause the least harm to students. Thank them for their support in the past, their understanding of the importance of the library media program, and your confidence that funding will be restored in next year's budget. Resist the temptation to threaten to tear them limb from limb or to support school board candidates in the next school election who would fire them all.

BOARD OF EDUCATION

The board of education makes the decisions in the broadest sense on how district education funds will be allocated in the district. After that, district and building administrators make program, funding, and staffing decisions.

In some districts the board may make the decision on how many library media specialists will staff each media center. They may also arrive at a total district figure for media center materials and equipment and allocate that amount among the schools in the district, perhaps on a per-pupil basis.

Whatever method is used in your district, you should know how budgeting works. It is clear that members of the board of education (or whatever that group of district-level decision makers is called) have some say in how your library media center is funded. The serious competition for limited dollars places pressure on board members from building administrators, the pupil personnel people, the athletics departments, the performing arts, and all other areas. You need to make sure that the needs of an excellent library media program do not get lost in the shuffle. You and other media specialists in the district must ensure that board members:

- know the role and function of the library media program

- understand how the library media program contributes to the education of youngsters

- recognize that a professional library media specialist and support staff are essential in implementing the program.

GET TO KNOW THE BOARD MEMBERS

In districts where there is a district library media coordinator, much of the information to the board will come from that office. Furthermore, regulations in your district may restrict your direct access to board members. Learn the protocol in your district and follow it. For example, rather than sending flyers and reports directly to board members, you may have to send them to the district office for distribution. Nevertheless, you should know each board member. They should recognize you, what you do, and how you interact with teachers and students. Since you are probably the only library media specialist in your building and one of a relatively small group in your district (unlike foreign language or first-grade teachers), it is easier for you and board members to become acquainted.

In small, geographically compact school districts, getting to know the board members is not difficult. It is much harder in a district that serves a metropolitan area or that covers many square miles with a district office far removed from where you work. Regardless of your district's size, however, you still need to channel information to them about the library media center and its program. Use the mail, the phone, the fax, interschool delivery, and your computer network to communicate with board members.

Often, newly elected board members begin their terms knowing little about various educational programs in the district. This is a prime time to reach out and educate them about the library media center mission. You may want to develop a plan with other library media specialists in the district to carry this out, but do not assume that your individual, personal efforts are no longer needed even though it's a group effort. Each media specialist in the district should be striving to make the library media program highly visible to the board members, both newly elected and long-time incumbents.

Don't give up if there are few or no responses. Persistence does pay off in the long run. Susan D. Ballard of the Londonderry (NH) School District reported a success story in *Gotta Have a Gimmick*:

> We had been trying for three years in a row to hire a third elementary school library media specialist so that each of our schools at that level would have full-time professional service. We had come close to realizing our goal, but kept getting put on the back burner. A new member was appointed to the school board and during his first time through the budget process, had so much information to absorb, that we felt sure he would not be able to get

to the level of understanding we had achieved with at least two other members of the board. However, we had not counted on the fact that he dutifully read his entire school board packet and that meant he read *Media Matters* [the Department of Library Media Services quarterly publication]. Enough so, that he apparently discussed some of our information with parents, teachers and principals.

The day of the big budget show-down came and the Superintendent of Schools informed the board that he had only included three new positions in the budget out of 28 requests. All new personnel were in the area of special education. Everyone in the audience looked at the members of the library media department for our reaction. It looked like we were on hold again when the new member of the board spoke up. Out of his mouth came phrases like "effective users of ideas and information" and the "library media specialist has three distinct roles: teacher, information specialist and instructional consultant." We were shocked! It was the first time EVER that we just got to listen as someone else explained to the good people of our community what a school library media specialist does. He made a motion to also include this vital position for funding, got an immediate second from another board member who noted "the library is a classroom, too . . . the most important in the school." It was a 3 to 2 vote in favor! PR works when you least expect it! (American Library Association 1993, p. 34)

It is impossible to overemphasize that all our efforts are focused on improving the education of the children in our districts. We are not empire builders, we are not in a race to get a bigger budget than someone else, nor are we trying to increase our own importance. We are advocating for library media programs from which all the children in the school district will benefit.

Here are some ideas you may consider using to help you get to know board members, to inform them, and to enlist their support of the district's library media program.

SEEK SUPPORT

- In cooperation with other library media specialists in the district prepare a sound-slide or videotape program on the role of the library media center and the media specialist in the instructional program. Present it at a board of education meeting and distribute flyers on media center services. Include pictures of lots of kids in the presentation. This is a child-centered presentation, not one focused on how hard you work, how understaffed or short of funds you are.

- What percentage of the school district budget is spent on library materials? Create a presentation for a board of education meeting to deliver during the budget process.

- Figure out how many books per student can be purchased with the library budget allocation. You are in a very unusual district if the budget covers the purchase of one book per student in the district, but this is not an unreasonable goal to press for. If they have never done this arithmetic, the board members will probably be amazed at how few books the amount will purchase. You may need to stress that all the technology available does not preclude the need for books to help form the reading habit and ensure enduring literacy.

- Encourage parents to attend board meetings and at appropriate times to speak in support of media center programs in the district.

- Why do you need to purchase new materials every year? Consider new media and technology and how it benefits learning; replacement of out-of-date materials; changes in curriculum; change in the characteristics of the student body (ESL students, special education students); new state regulations. Let board members know how these factors impact your budget. Don't assume that they just naturally consider these linkages.

COMMUNICATE OFTEN

- Write a note to the president of the board describing the dedication of an excellent teacher or administrator in your building. Choose someone, of course, who is supportive of the media center program.

- Put board of education meetings on your calendar and attend as often as you can. Encourage other media specialists in the district to attend, also. Always be there at budget time. Your very presence may cause a late-night search for a plan that by-passes cuts in the library media program. It has happened!

- Speak to the board members during the social time before the meeting begins. Make sure they know your name and that you are the media specialist in your school. Always be positive. Whiners get tuned out.

- During National Library Week or School Library Media Month, send letters to board members reinforcing the national emphasis on libraries at that time. Outline the role of library media programs in the educational process of students. Thank them for their support.

- Send copies of your reports, newsletters, and other publications to board members.

- How does your library media center measure up against state, regional, national standards? How do award-winning media centers differ from yours? The news could be bad, which indicates unmet needs and an increase in funding. It could be good, for which you will want to thank the decision makers. Let board members know either way. Don't let a visiting evaluation team be the ones who inform the board that your library is below standards. It would ruin you.

- You received an increase in funding, another support-staff position, approval for expanding your facility? Be sure to write thank-you letters to the board members.

VOLUNTEER TO HELP

- Volunteer to do a presentation on library media centers at the regional, state, or national conferences of the school board associations. You can approach the association through your own board members or through your state or national library media organization.

- Write an article on some unique aspect or application of library media for the journal of the state or national school board association.

INVITE VISITS

- Issue a standing invitation to board of education members to visit the media center whenever they are in your building.

- Invite board members to read at an annual Read-a-Thon.

- Join with the library media specialists in the district and invite board of education members to a candlelight dinner in the media center. If you can, include district administrators. Ask student volunteers to help serve, provide music, and act as tour guides.

- Invite board members to visit your library media center when you initiate a new computer service. Inform the media of this event and be sure that board members are photographed.

- Invite board members to a breakfast in the media center. Display many types of material, provide handouts, and have students there to conduct tours.

- Ask the president of the board to introduce an author who is the speaker at the program in your media center, or to award the prizes at a media center competition.

- Invite a board member who is especially supportive of the library media program to speak at a meeting of your library media association. One of the things the association members may want to know is what the board member sees as the most effective ways to get the library media message across.

WIN FRIENDS

- Write letters to candidates for board of education positions wishing them well in their campaigns and seeking their support for library media centers. Whether they win or lose, they can become friends of the library media program.

- After the election, write congratulatory notes to the winners and offer media center services that may help them in their new positions.

- Congratulate board members who are re-elected and thank them for their support in the past.

- Develop a display of hobbies and hobby books. Ask board of education members to include information about their hobbies.

- Send birthday greeting cards to board members and include a list of other "celebrities" who have the same birth date.

- Include board members in a display of photographs of people and their favorite books, authors, or reading material. Invite them to see the display. Take photographs and write an article for the district newsletter about this display.

- When your library media center program is recognized or honored in some way (e.g., designated as an "electronic doorway" by the state), ask that the certificate be presented at a board of education meeting by an official from the organization making the award. Having someone from an "outside" agency lends greater credence and recognition. Of course, display the certificate in a prominent place in the media center. This is an excellent photo opportunity.

- In honor of School Board Recognition Week, ask school board members to select a book (or topic) of their choice. Solicit funds from the Friends of the Library Media Center to purchase these books, which are then dedicated in the board members' names. Each book should bear a bookplate that honors the member for his/her service to the school district.

- Ask the president of the board of education to issue a proclamation declaring School Library Media Week and urging the school community to use school library media services.

- At a ceremony during National Library Week or Love the Board of Education Week, present board members with "gold" library cards. This makes a good photo opportunity.

Chapter 6

PARENTS AND OTHER COMMUNITY FRIENDS: PARTNERS IN EDUCATION

PARENTS

Parents should be our strongest allies as we seek support to maintain, improve, and expand library media programs. After all, their children benefit directly from an excellent library media program. As people who are deeply committed to our work, we care about the youngsters we deal with on a daily basis and are concerned deeply about those youngsters who can't or won't read. We want kids to learn and feel comfortable using information skills, which will affect their lives forever. It is essential that we get this message over to parents. By reaching out to parents, we reach children.

Too many parents, however, don't know what goes on in the library media center. Nor do they know what our jobs are. Few have even a faint idea of the central role that the library media program plays in their children's education, and no one is likely to inform them if we fail to deliver the message.

Unlike some of our other audiences, we do not interact with parents every day. They may come to Open School Night and stop by the library media center. They may attend meetings of the parent-faculty organization where you happen to be the speaker, but these organizations are not always strong, meetings are often poorly attended, and experience tells us that as youngsters move into the upper grades, fewer and fewer of their parents participate in such organizations. When parents come to conferences with their children's teachers, it is unlikely that we have the opportunity to see them.

Youngsters whose parents are involved in their children's learning get higher grades and stay in school longer. Parents can affect student learning through their attitudes, values, the variety of reading materials in the home, and the limits they place on their youngsters' television viewing. In fact, "when parents are involved in a variety of ways at school, the performance of all children in the school tends to improve" (U.S. Dept. of Education 1996, p. 7).

PARENTS AS LIBRARY SUPPORTERS

When parents understand the library media center's function, they can become strong sources of support. They will speak out at school district meetings and budget hearings, they will appear before the board of education to voice their concerns about libraries, they will visit building and district administrators to advocate for the library media program. They will write letters to state legislators and give testimony before legislative education committees urging greater state funding for library media centers. They will write letters to local newspapers. They will become involved because they care about the education of their children. As private citizens, they can play a big part in bringing about substantive change.

Parents have a powerful voice in demanding a better education for their children, the users of our services. Their messages carry much greater weight than our own because we may be perceived as serving our own interests. Support from vocal parents is invaluable as we seek to improve the library media program and services that mean so much in their children's education.

How can we reach parents? Here are some ideas that you may want to consider—or that may spark ideas of your own.

OPEN SCHOOL NIGHT

- For Open School Night, or whatever the open house event is called in your district, prepare a video or sound-slide presentation showing how the library media center is an integral part of youngsters' education (see Figure 6–1).

- Put out flyers that include information on how the media center staff works with students, hours the media center is open, and a list of staff members, including volunteers. Give some examples of original thinking or activities by students in which the media center played a role.

- Provide tours of the media center conducted by students.

- Have students at computers to show what the computers (and the kids) can do.

- Make available bookmarks for parents that recommend books on parenting.

- Encourage parents to check out books on the students' cards.

Figure 6–1 Open School Invitation to Parents

NOTICE
TO
~~CUSTOMERS~~ PARENTS

B.S.H.S. LIBRARY MEDIA CENTER
INVITES YOU

to visit us on

Open School Night

October 25

Come in, say "Hello," and look over our
computer services, books, magazines, video
and audiotape collections, art reproductions,
and much, much more!

FREE

Reading Lists

Brochures

Guided Tours

- Set up a bulletin board on "Wonderful Things to Do in the Library Media Center," with photographs of students doing them (see Figure 2–1).

- Organize your student volunteers to baby-sit in the school building for the event.

- Prepare name tags for staff and student volunteers to wear.

- Have parents sign a Guest List. Send them a "thank you for coming" note.

- Put out lots of book displays—how to study, books on how to prepare for PSATs, how to pay for college, choosing a college, and the like.

- Hold your annual book fair during the week that Open School Night is scheduled. Help parents select books for their children. Prepare flyers on how parents can help their youngsters become better readers.

COMMUNICATION WITH PARENTS

- With the first report-card mailing of the school year, enclose a flyer to parents on how the media center helps students.

- Write notes to parents of students who have done something "positive." Develop a greeting card format for this congratulatory note.

- Clip and send parents newspaper items about good things their children have done. This is a good job for a volunteer.

- Encourage a student to write an article for the school publication that goes home to the parents. The student point of view offers a fresh perspective on library media center activities and services.

- Write an article each month on library media center activities for the school newsletter that goes to parents.

- Include in each newsletter an annotated bibliography on books and articles about parenting, issues in education, and youngsters. Keep it short.

- Prepare a guide to the media center that includes services the media specialists provide, services for the faculty, information about the collection, a list of information retrieval services available, services to the community, and a floor plan. Distribute this to faculty members, also.

- If your district publishes a calendar that goes to all parents, make sure that National Library Week, School Library Media Month, book fairs, the Read-a-Thon, and other annual library events are included in it.

FAMILY READING

- Plan an annual Family Reading Night in your school. Invite parents and their children to come to the media center to read aloud. Set out displays and handouts on the advantages of reading together.

- With the public library, plan a workshop for parents on how they can encourage their children to read for pleasure. Encourage a tradition of family "read alouds" in families with school-age children.

- With the public library staff, produce for parents a list of good read-aloud books for children of different ages. Distribute copies in both the school and public libraries.

- Heavy television viewing by children cuts down the time they spend on acquiring basic reading and writing skills. Present a workshop for parents, perhaps in cooperation with the public library, on how they can alter their children's viewing habits:

  — limit the number of hours they allow their children to spend watching TV

  — be aware of what their children watch

  — insist that children finish their homework before they turn on TV

  — watch TV with their children

  — eat dinner together with the TV off

  — let their children see them reading books, magazines, and newspapers more and watching TV less. Being a good role model is a powerful influence. Parents or primary-care givers who are readers are cited in research as the number-one motivating force for children who embrace a lifelong reading habit.

INVOLVE PARENTS

- Organize a Friends of the Library for your school. Work with parents on ways in which they can be advocates for the library media program and activities. Invite students, faculty, staff, and community residents to become members.

- Invite parents who come to school for conferences with their children's teachers to stop by the media center for a look around and some refreshments.

- Be on the lookout for parents who would like to be library volunteers.

- Encourage parents to participate in library media center Read-a-Thons.

- Offer parents the use of such media center equipment as the laminator, transparency maker, and video copier for their home-produced videos. These are jobs your trained student volunteers can assist with.

- Encourage parent groups to donate ongoing funding to the library media center to cover the cost of a specific resource (e.g., *Sirs* on CD-ROM). Be sure to thank the group in the school's newsletter to parents.

- Invite parents of high-school seniors to honor their graduating youngsters with a donation to the library media center collection. Remind them that the students' names will be included on the bookplates in the materials purchased.

- Include parents and other community members in any ceremony in the library media center in which students are awarded special recognitions or prizes. Have photographers present.

- Keep a list of expensive books and other materials the budget does not cover. If the parents' group offers a gift to the media center, ask them to select a title or titles from the list according to the amount of the gift or the subject that interests them. If they do not think of presenting a gift, find a channel through which the suggestion can be made.

PARENT-FACULTY ORGANIZATION

- Become an active member of the parent-faculty organization in your school.

- Volunteer to serve on a committee in the parent-faculty organization.

- Report at each meeting on what's happening in the library media center.

- Volunteer to speak to the group about such topics as the role of the school library program, how parents can foster their youngsters' enjoyment of reading, the new technology in the media center and how youngsters benefit, your plans for the upcoming year, and your budget requests.

- Screen a video or sound-slide presentation about what goes on in the media center. Include lots of kids!

- Invite parent groups in the school to hold their meetings in the media center. Attend some of the meetings, display materials, have flyers for parents to pick up.

- Prepare flyers, bookmarks, or some other handout to give parents at each meeting. They can present information useful to parents, short bibliographies, books parents can read to their children, or some seasonal information. Emphasis should be on the kids, parents, and the media center.

- Put up a small media center display at each meeting.

THE WIDER AUDIENCE

- Write articles about school libraries for such general magazines as *Better Homes and Gardens, Good Housekeeping*, and *Parents* that carry articles each month on education. Emphasize the importance to children's education of a well-supported library media center program that is staffed by professional library media specialists. Quote research that supports your statements.

- Read education articles in popular magazines that are read by parents. Do they include the importance of excellent, well-staffed library media programs when evaluating schools? Write letters to editors supporting what the articles report or supplying information about library media programs when they fail to include it. You will have increased the awareness of editors and their readers either way.

SUBSTITUTE TEACHERS

A very small segment of the residents of the community is that group of people who work as substitute teachers in the schools. They come into the schools frequently, unlike other community members, and they are much more aware than other people in the community of what goes on in the classrooms and the media center. They bring classes to the media center, they are involved with the media specialist in instructional planning, and they substitute for you in the media center when you're away. Some substitute teachers who find themselves working in the media center discover that it is an area that they like very much, and they go on to become library media specialists.

The substitute teacher is in a position to speak knowledgeably about the library media program and the important role it plays in the education of the community's children. The subs are people whom we as media specialists should get to know better and whom we should recruit to speak for the media center program in the community.

Here are some ways to win friends to the library media program from among substitute teachers.

WELCOME BUILDING SUBS

- Make up a folder of materials for substitute teachers. Give copies to the front office so they can pass it on. Put in it information that perhaps the front office has not told them: photocopying policy and location of copiers; a list of books in the media center collection that contain instant lesson plans for substitutes to use in classes for which teachers did not leave plans; lists of books with puzzles and good books to read aloud.

- Get to know the substitute teachers who come to your building, invite them to sit with you at lunch, introduce them to other teachers, make them feel welcome.

- Offer substitute teachers in your building a spot in which to work or relax. Give them access to your coffee pot.

PLAN FOR YOUR SUB

- Leave good plans for the substitute who covers for you when you are absent. Make her feel welcome, let her know where the things she will need are located, and try to schedule a light class day for her. Keep on your desk a folder of general library information for the sub in case you are unexpectedly absent.

- Maintain a "Projects to Do" folder so you can quickly come up with jobs that need to be done in case classes are not heavily scheduled on the day you are absent. Be sure to include clear instructions for doing the tasks.

- School district policies vary, but if possible, request a sub who has done a good job in your position in the past. There seem to be few subs who are media specialists, but some have special talents that make them very useful in the library media center. A knowledgeable, effective substitute who relates well to teachers, students, and media center staff is a plus for the media center program.

MAINTAIN CONTACT

- Suggest to the teachers that together you organize plans for library research activities for substitutes to use when teachers are away. The substitute teachers will be grateful for concrete plans (they don't want to be baby-sitters), and teachers will know their classes are actively involved in learning when they are absent.

- Put substitute teachers on your distribution list for flyers, newsletters, and other media center publications.

COMMUNITY MEMBERS

The residents of your community pay the largest portion of the funding needed to operate the public schools. For schools to carry out their missions they need the good will, understanding, and support of the community.

Adults with no children now in the schools form the largest bloc of taxpayers in many communities. Although most of them know that the cost of ignorance to society far outstrips the taxes they pay to support the schools, some, in this era of closer scrutiny of tax-supported institutions, look on the public schools as an expense they no longer care to indulge. Since the law requires schools, these disaffected people search for ways to cut the costs of operating them. They find many programs that they label "frills," among them school nurses, the lunch program, driver education, art and music programs, and the library media program.

While central office officials work hard to keep the community enfranchised, they must also emphasize the total education program in the district. They seldom focus on a specific program such as the library media center, so this responsibility, if it is to be carried out, falls to the individual library media specialist or specialists in the district. We must explain, justify, and enlist community support for library media center programs.

Members of the community, especially those whose children are no longer in school, may have very little understanding of or interest in where the school library media program fits into the overall educational picture or of the need for a professional staff to implement the program. They are often unaware of what the media specialist does, and if asked would reply that "He checks out books." (How often have you been asked if you had to go to college to do your job, or worse, had someone express amazement that you went to college?) There is an appalling lack of knowledge that we must deal with if we are to create favorable opinion and support for library media programs. This calls for persistence on our part. One well-meant effort during National Library Week is not enough. There must be ongoing outreach to get the message through. (One way can even be through your car—see Figure 6–2.)

VOLUNTEERS

Volunteering in the library media center provides adults an opportunity to play a role in carrying out the mission of the school. Those who have retired from full-time employment sometimes feel the need to be involved in a worthwhile community activity and seek an opportunity to keep in contact with others. Many look forward to the interaction they have with students and enjoy being with youngsters.

Volunteers who come into the library and see the activities that take place there are in a position to understand how vital the media center is to the educational process. People who become part of library projects and activities are likely to become library media center supporters because, through their involvement, they develop a sense of ownership. We must strive to make volunteers feel that they are important to the organization. They give to the media center program something more valuable than money: they give of themselves, of their time. We can recognize their services and how they impact on student learning through reports, publications, and speeches, particularly in the local community.

Volunteers can take over tasks that release the library media specialist to spend more time on professional responsibilities. They can also relieve clerical workers of

---

Figure 6–2 Vanity License Plates

A baker's dozen vanity plates to consider the next time you get a car license plate:

ILOV BKS

BKS 4 US

BKS R ME

BKS4UNME

BKS 4 U

BKS4 ALL

READMORE

READ BKS

INFOTOGO

INFO4ALL

ILUVINFO

INFO4YOU

READGROW

---

routine tasks, thus making them available for more demanding jobs. Some of the tasks volunteers perform are services to teachers and students that might never be done were they not there to do them. They can give one-on-one attention to students who might otherwise not get any.

To help volunteers feel comfortable in the library media center, in the building, and with the tasks you have assigned them, create a folder for each one filled with information about media center services, policies, floor plans of the center and of the building, phone numbers of whom to call in case of absence, and a list of names and number of all media center volunteers. As they take notes on how to do the various jobs, they can add these to their folders.

Sometime during the school year (in the doldrums of late January, perhaps), designate a special day to honor community members who volunteer in the library media center. Plan an after-school party for the volunteers, serve refreshments, invite administrators and faculty, and ask the principal to speak to the group about the contribution of the volunteers. You may want to include others in your planning and focus on all the volunteers who work in the building. Write an article for the district newspaper and include photographs of the volunteers. Volunteers give of their time, a precious commodity, and it is important that they are aware of your appreciation.

Following are some of the many jobs community volunteers can do.

Maintain Library Collections and Records

— Help with inventory.

— Clip or photocopy items the librarian has marked for the vertical file.

— Maintain the vertical file. Refile, make new folders, replace labels, discard old materials.

— Shift materials to make more shelf space available.

— Shelve returned materials and keep shelves in order.

— Remove discarded and lost materials from library records.

— Repair battered books.

Process Orders and Materials

— Check in new magazines, put them into plastic folders, prepare back issues for circulation, keep the collection of back files in order.

— Maintain the collection of materials that arrive on a weekly or monthly basis.

— Help prepare new materials for use.

— Attach clear plastic covers to book jackets.

— Check orders of new materials against order forms.

Help Teachers

— Gather and photocopy articles from a list the librarian selects for a teacher's project.

— Gather and process materials to place on reserve for teachers' classes based on lists the librarian makes up.

Other Library Media Tasks

— Process interlibrary loan requests.

— Input data into the computer.

— Work on bulletin boards and displays.

— Photocopy, collate, fold, and staple flyers, reports, bibliographies, and other materials.

— Distribute materials to teachers' mailboxes, gather and sort mail from the library box.

— Read aloud to students.

— Work at the circulation desk.

VOLUNTEERS AS LIBRARY SUPPORTERS

Volunteers can become goodwill ambassadors to the community as they talk to their friends about the positive things they see happening in "their" media center. They are in a good position to refute the statements of those who want to see media center budgets slashed and staffs reduced so as to lower their tax rates.

As I've pointed out before, media specialists need people from the community to speak up at board of education meetings and budget hearings for library media programs. We need them to write letters to the newspapers and other media in response to items in the news. Letters that support positive articles are just as important as those that provide information that corrects erroneous information.

We can invite community members to accompany us when we visit our legislators to seek moneys for school media center programs. Their more objective voices can speak to the effectiveness of library media programs in helping kids become better readers and better students.

Here are some activities that may be useful in keeping community members informed as you do your work to obtain and expand support from them.

ACTIVITIES

Communicate with the Community

- Volunteer to speak at service club meetings (Lions, Rotary, Women's Clubs, etc.). This is especially valuable near budget time, when people want to know why "all that money is being spent on libraries. I thought they bought books last year?" and, "Can't kids use the public library?" Be certain to respond fully and without rancor to these and other such questions.

- Get to know who on the local newspaper reports on education. Advise her well in advance of media center happenings she might want to report on.

- Find out when the local newspaper publishes its regular school information column or page. Be sure that you send in items about upcoming special events in the library media center.

- Keep and place in a scrapbook any print item that mentions the library media center. Send copies of all items to your principal and district administrators.

- Get to know the radio stations in your community. They broadcast calendars of events, public service announcements, and spot news, any of which you might use for promoting your school's media program activities. Learn the name of the station's contact person and what the station's requirements are. Gather all of this information so that you'll have it readily available when you need it.

- How many pennies per day do taxpayers spend on school library books and materials? Do this arithmetic and publish the information. How many books are purchased with the annual budget allotment for books in your school district? How much does this come to for each household in the district?

- Ask the school district PR person to focus on district library media programs in the district newspaper during School Library Media Month. You and other district media specialists can volunteer to help plan the issue and to provide ideas and photos for that issue.

- Use a rubber stamp and a red ink pad on all mailings that you send from the library. Select a stamp with a message about libraries, reading, or use the national library symbol. It's an easy way to give media centers visibility.

- Many people think "books" when they hear "library." To change this incomplete image, we must get the message to the community that instructional media includes any format that communicates information to users. Explain how different kinds of media are ideally suited to presenting particular kinds of information. Show how students and teachers use different media and how they benefit students educationally. Tie in the change in name from "library" to "library media center." Make the community aware of the broad range of resources required to convey information to today's students.

- Videotape students engaged in all kinds of activities in the media center. Arrange with businesses in the town to show the tapes during School Library Media Month. Approach a fast-food restaurant, a bank, a food store, or stores in the mall. Community members will pause in their shopping to see students they know, and they will also see the great things that take place in the media center.

- Develop a project with teachers in which students from several grade levels write about the library and what it means to them. Select several for use in a videotape that you show on Open House Night and when you speak to community and parent groups. You can also use the statements in pamphlet format.

- Consider calling into a radio talk show in your community. Mention the role school media centers play in children's education and the need for people to be aware of the benefits to youngsters. Be ready to answer questions (they may be tough ones) that the host will ask. Remain calm and positive no matter how negative a response you receive. Role play with another media specialist before you call.

- Join with other media specialists in the district to design (perhaps with an art teacher's help) a placemat with a message about library media centers. Clear the project with administrators and the district public relations person, and arrange to distribute them to local restaurants to be used during School Library Media Month.

Invite Involvement

- Early in the school year let the community know that you would welcome volunteers. Schedule an orientation session where you talk about the jobs they might do and what their contribution would mean to the library media center program and to youngsters.

- Invite community members to read in your annual Read-a-Thon or on other less formal occasions. Include grandparents and other senior citizens in this undertaking.

- Invite community groups to meet in the media center after school hours.

- Invite town and community officials to special events in the media center. These make good photo opportunities for them and your media center.

- Ask an outspoken critic of expenditures for the library media center program to volunteer a few hours a week so he can see the activities that go on there. You just may win him over.

Involve Yourself

- Volunteer to write articles about library media activities for the superintendent's weekly column in the local newspaper.

- Ask the superintendent to invite you to appear on his weekly radio and/or TV program.

- Prepare for the local paper a list of books students might enjoy receiving for Christmas or other holidays. Include short annotations and reading levels.

- Arrange to take a group of children to visit a nursing home or senior residence. Prepare the group to tell stories, read aloud, present a short play.

- Get to know the public information person in your school district. Be sure that he includes information about media centers in official releases from the district. Volunteer to serve on the district public information advisory committee.

- Enter a float with a library theme in the annual Memorial Day parade, the parade opening the Little League season, the Christmas parade, or some other parade in your town. If the project seems overwhelming, get media specialists from other schools to join you. Have lots of kids on the float. Be sure photos get in the paper. Get someone from the newspaper or the TV station to come to the float-building session.

- With your county school and public library associations, plan for a booth for a county fair containing exhibits showing school and public library services and the ways the members of the community benefit from our services. Demonstrate electronic information sources. Many nonlibrary users think of libraries as they were a hundred years ago. They will be amazed by the CD-ROMs, computers, Internet sources, and other up-to-date ways that information can be accessed. This might be a project for regional library systems to sponsor.

- Discuss with the continuing education coordinator in the district offering a course to teach parents and grandparents how to help their children become better readers.

Form Coalitions

- Get to know leaders of such groups as Girl and Boy Scouts, Head Start, 4H, etc. Work with them to develop reading lists and library media activities. Establishing alliances and collaborating with other youth-services groups expands the potential for improving library services to youngsters.

- Let grandparents, parents, and other community members know you welcome library volunteers.

Other Libraries

- Develop a close working relationship with public library staff. Let them know about teachers' assignments as you learn about them. Work collaboratively with them to involve parents and other adults with children's reading and technology.

- Contact the director of your local college library and find out what its policies are regarding your students using their materials.

- Take a moonlighting job for a few hours a week (or volunteer) at the public library. You'll see students in a different setting (and they will see you). You get to know community people, become acquainted with public library staff; you see and use books and material that you may want to add to the media center collection; and they even pay you while you're getting all of these benefits. Community people get to know you, too.

- Invite public library staff members to visit the media center to see how the other half lives and works. Ask them to do booktalks now and then in your media center.

- Meet with your public librarian to talk about common problems, shared joys, and especially opportunities to ensure that both school and public library services are seen as vital to youth development and the efforts of other youth and family-serving agencies.

- Share your media center newsletter, bibliographies, and other publications with your public library. Ask the public library director to send you the materials they produce.

- Make sure that you include in your messages to the community the need for both school and public library services. Point out that the specific mission of the school library media center is to support the educational program of the school. Schools and public libraries cooperate, both are necessary, but they have different emphases. Children need two types of libraries for the different purposes and time blocks they have.

- If the residents of your school attendance area do not have easy access to the public library, you may want to investigate with your administrators and the public library staff the possibility of the school library being open to the public some evenings. Staffing would be a public library responsibility, as would providing materials for adults. This could be a way of bringing library services to a group who do not have easy access, and families would bring their children with them. This would be an opportunity to encourage families to read together.

Chapter 7

LEGISLATORS AND OTHER OFFICIALS: THE "AYES" HAVE IT

So far in our discussion of public relations for library media programs, we have been concerned with promoting the use of and encouraging support for the media centers in which we work and for those in our own school district. Our efforts for school libraries, however, must extend beyond our district boundaries to libraries in districts across the state and throughout the nation, as well as to libraries outside of schools.

These days, services in all libraries are interconnected, and all need support. We need to keep a global view and work to improve all libraries in the state and nation. It is especially important to set our sights beyond our own operations when we are dealing with decision makers at the state and federal levels. When library services for kids everywhere make gains from state and federal decisions, then too do youngsters in our own schools.

Beyond the decision makers who are employed by our own school district and the local boards of education, there is a group whose decisions influence every area of our lives daily. Members of this group include those who are elected or appointed (or would like to be) to serve and represent us on local boards, county boards, and commissions; they represent us in the state capitols and in Washington, DC; they are employed in city, state, and federal agencies that deal with every aspect of our lives, including libraries and schools. These are people we want to have on the side of libraries, and it is our job to persuade them that kids really do need libraries, and that the services and resources of school and public libraries complement each other.

WHAT DECISION MAKERS DON'T KNOW

Libraries enjoy a unique status in their communities. They are loved by many who habitually use them; respected but ignored by many others who may not regard them as relevant to their lives. Someone has said that support for libraries is a mile wide and an inch deep. Some people love to tell us about going to the library as a youngster—Their eyes get moist and their voices catch as they recall the wonderful librarian who gave them their first library card and actually let them take books home! Oh, joy! For many, this is the sum total of their knowledge and experience in libraries. Once out of childhood, they apparently have never used libraries again, or don't remember if they did. They may, depending on their ages, have crossed the threshold of libraries in high school or college or graduate school. But there is certainly little emotional tug displayed toward libraries beyond that of the childhood library experience.

The point here, and you may be wondering if there is one, is that many people who make decisions about funding for libraries are not and never have been library users themselves to any great extent, and really don't understand what all the fuss is about. Okay, we need books for children in public libraries, but why do we need to duplicate efforts for kids in public schools? Aren't school libraries branches of public libraries? Don't librarians from public libraries stop by school libraries from time to time to read to the children? Isn't this what a school library is? Why do little children need a professional, highly paid librarian to do that job? Can't mothers take turns coming to school to read to the children? They may never actually ask us these questions, but as we talk with them about library issues and needs for library services, we sense that these are the questions going through their minds. We talk on one level about libraries; they listen on another, filtering what they hear through their own meager experiences, half-understandings, and misconceptions. They do not see effective library media programs as having a positive impact on student learning.

There is a true story about a media specialist who wrote to a governor seeking his support for a regulation requiring a professional media specialist in every school media center. The governor's cordial but neutral response was a great disappointment, not only for his lack of position on the issue, but also because he wrote (if indeed, he wrote the letter—probably an aide did) of his lifelong affection for public libraries. Later, in personal contact with the governor, the librarian confirmed that the governor did not comprehend that school and public libraries are different entities with different goals and missions. In light of this, one can appreciate why he didn't take a position on the issue before him. We need to clarify in our own minds the goals and missions of each type of library and give concrete examples of results achieved by each for meeting children's different needs at different times. We must explain that, like adults who utilize public, research, and college libraries for different purposes at different times, young people also need complementary services.

LIBRARIES—MORE THAN BOOKS

People who have had little experience in libraries in recent years associate libraries only with books. Although the print and broadcast media are filled with references to the information highway, the information age, and the multiplicity of new formats, many people do not connect all of these with libraries. What some legislators and other political decision makers know about libraries is on a par with what Marie Antoinette knew about starving people.

This is not meant to make any group of people look bad. If anyone comes off looking less than perfect, it is librarians. Just because we know what our job is, and because regular library users know the services libraries provide, we cannot assume that everyone else does. It is up to us to apprise decision makers of libraries' many services and how, specifically, people use them; and what large benefits accrue from these uses.

Adding to this problem is the public's ignorance of how schools and teaching have moved away from textbooks toward resource-based instruction. The impact of this change on library media centers and the people who staff them has brought about a whole new world. How kids use media centers today bears little resemblance to media center activities of fifteen years, or even ten years, ago—not to mention thirty to forty years ago, when some or most of the present-day influential decision makers were youngsters. The high-school libraries that they remember from their youth may have been little more than study halls.

OTHER OFFICIALS AND INFLUENTIAL PEOPLE

People in the state education department, members of the state board of education, the state commissioner of education, the governor—and the list goes on and on. All should hear from us about how essential school library media programs are in the education of today's children and tomorrow's adults. We cannot assume that the people holding these prestigious positions are as fully cognizant of libraries as they need to be to make thoughtful and accurate decisions about library policies and funding. We must put information into their hands.

Call-in-show hosts, news commentators, TV talk-show hosts, and others in the broadcast media make decisions about the items that will be given air time on their programs. How often do they mention negative things about education? When they do, and it is frequently, they inadvertently open up for us opportunities to speak about the need for strong library media programs and how these programs can benefit kids. No one can do this better than we can.

There are those who hold no office, who do not appear before large audiences, but who work behind the scenes wielding influence with officials and other prominent people. Such individuals may be in business, in a social position, in the arts or entertainment, or feel the need to make a contribution in this manner. Conveying your concepts and enthusiasms to someone who has the ear of decision makers can provide you with a channel for your own message. Get to know who these people are.

Listed here are some strategies for getting the attention of decision makers as well as some techniques that have proven to be effective in communicating with them.

ACTIVITIES

GET TO KNOW YOUR LEGISLATORS

- Get to know your representative in the state legislature and work to develop a personal rapport.

- Learn about your district's representative. What is her party, her pet projects, her position (if any) on library issues? Does she have a special relationship with library services—a disabled child, a blind father who uses special library equipment?

- Develop rapport with the legislator's office staff who arrange appointments. Know the names of the secretaries and legislative aides. Write their names in your address book and speak to them by name when you call the office and visit.

- Get to know those serving on your state association's legislative committee. Attend the sessions they sponsor at annual state conferences.

LEARN THE ROPES

- Keep up with and become an expert on legislation that concerns you. Your state library media association legislative committee can help you learn how to monitor the progress of legislation.

- Learn to be a lobbyist, one who works to influence a legislator to vote a certain way on a piece of legislation. Here again your state association will teach you how.

- Do your homework! Don't ask your legislator to support legislation if he or she is already a sponsor of the legislation. The legislator will think that you are uninformed about legislative procedure. Instead, thank him for his support.

- Ask to be put on a mailing list to receive information about public hearings and the status of legislation.

- Know who serves on the committees writing legislation that concerns you, and the names of committee staffers.

- Read articles about state and federal library legislation in your state association's publications and in those of the American Library Association. Tie in with someone or a group that subscribes to the ALA Washington office news channels.

- Find out about the ALA Washington office and ask them for information on congressional legislation. As of 1995 an ALA staff member has been assigned to monitor school library and other youth service matters.

- Attend legislative workshops at the ALA Annual Conference as well as those at the conferences of the American Association of School Librarians.

- Find out if your state association sponsors a library legislative day in the state capitol when people from across the state gather to visit their representatives to discuss library issues. This is a great time to learn the ropes if you are new to the game.

- Plan to attend an ALA annual legislative day in Washington held usually during National Library Week.

- Candidates for public office choose to run because they see issues they feel must be addressed, and they come from all sectors of the population. As an elected official you could make an impact on local, state, or national library policy. Consider being a candidate for office in your town, county, state, or at the national level.

TELL—AND SHOW—THEM THAT LIBRARIES BENEFIT PEOPLE

- Not only do we want to know the legislator, but we want him to know us and what we do. He needs to know that school and public libraries are different entities and that, although they both serve children and young people, their focuses differ. Having this and other information about libraries will help him understand how legislation will impact on library services to his constituents.

- Let him know what your library media center does and how important the program is to youngsters' educational achievement, their attitudes, perspectives, and personal goals.

- Let your legislator know how funding will benefit the children, the libraries, and the constituents in her district. Provide specific information about how individuals have effectively used library media services, and how libraries have made a difference in their lives. Anecdotal evidence can be very compelling.

- Gather support for library legislation by asking parents, community members, teachers, and administrators to write about specific instances when their children have benefited from library media services or suffered from the lack of it. Collect these anecdotal letters and hand deliver them to the legislative committee chairs concerned with library legislation. Ask other library media specialists to join you in this project. Expand it by including your school library system or your regional or state library media association. Presenting several thousand letters to the committee carries considerable impact.

WRITE AND COMMUNICATE

- Send individually typed letters expressing your concerns. Do not use printed or photocopied letters.

- Keep your letters brief and to the point, on one piece of legislation. If you haven't reduced your proposal to less than a page, you haven't yet worked it all out in your mind. Be sure your name, address, and phone and fax numbers are clear. Also include your E-mail address if you have one.

- Send telegrams, mailgrams, or E-mail to reinforce letters you have previously written about specific legislation.

- If elected officials in your state have radio call-in shows to keep in touch with the public, be one of the callers. Ask about library issues that have not been dealt with, or express your pleasure for the positive action taken. Be polite, hopeful, and never threatening.

- Petitions and post cards portray cheapness on your part and are considered least effective by legislators.

- Some legislators consider telephone calls ineffective. They also have a negative opinion of massive fax campaigns that tie up their equipment. They will strip their equipment from time to time and never see the messages that were on it.

- When bills you are interested in have passed the legislature, find out if they are likely to be signed by the governor. Do you and others need to write the governor, send telegrams, or make calls urging her to sign?

MEET AND SPEAK

- When the legislator comes to your community for a fund raiser or to give a speech, go to the function and speak to him; identify yourself and write a letter to him afterward about the meeting. You don't want your legislator to think that the only time you want to see him is when you want something from him. If you do something for him, such as come to one of his meetings, he may be more inclined to do something for you, such as support legislation you're interested in. After all, this is the political process.

- Sign up to testify before legislative committees. Your state association can let you know when and where committees will be holding hearings. Sign up early.

- Consider taking several articulate youngsters when you go to the state capitol to present testimony. Help the children prepare short statements, in their own words, about why library services are important to them.

- Take along copies of your testimony when you testify for the committee members, the press, and others. Sometimes the committees specify that they want you to leave twenty to thirty copies of your testimony. State your position clearly, and be sure that your testimony specifies how the legislation will benefit kids, adults, and the community.

- Talk about libraries to candidates for office. Attend political rallies. Ask questions about a candidate's position on library issues, and if he is uninformed, make it your job to provide him with information. If you cannot persuade him, support someone else.

- Invite your legislator, or other elected official, to a breakfast to talk about library issues. Ask other media specialists and your public librarian to participate in planning and running the meeting. You may want to suggest that your regional library media association sponsor an annual legislators' breakfast. A Saturday is a good time for that.

VISIT OFFICES

- Call to make an appointment and visit your legislator's local office two, three, or four times a year.

- By visiting your legislator frequently, you project yourself as the concerned and sincere person you are. Frequent visits give you and library issues visibility. Infrequent visits at crisis times probably come after the legislator's position is set.

- Visit your state legislator in his office at the state capitol. Make an appointment before you go, and take one or two people from the district with you— never more than four people at one time.

- Send information to the legislator before you visit.

- Have a plan of action for your group's meeting. Perhaps one person will speak and the others will provide additional information. Be sure you have a unified message. Legislators will be turned off completely if presented with conflicting views. They will think the library community doesn't know what it wants and use this as a reason to do nothing to help.

- Be prompt, but be prepared to wait.

- Choose as your spokesperson someone knowledgeable who can sum up a relatively complex issue in thirty seconds in language that is easy to understand.

- Be friendly and polite. Do not allow yourself to become argumentative and antagonistic toward anyone, even if the legislator and staff members are not especially helpful or supportive of your requests. Be prepared for rejection.

- Never threaten to campaign against a legislator even if you intend to vote against him.

- Leave materials with the legislator or staff member. Leave your name, address, phone and fax numbers, and your E-mail address. Attribute the legislator's negative position to his lack of understanding of the issue, and make it your job to inform him. Send him a copy of anything you have written about it.

- When visiting a legislator's office, ask to see a legislative counselor or aide if the legislator is not available. Aides serve an important role in bringing your message to the attention of the legislator, and will advocate for it if they are convinced. Make sure the aide or counselor knows who you are and the bills you are supporting, as well as those you do not support, and why.

- Always be positive when speaking with elected officials. They hear so many disaster stories that they recognize them immediately and tune them out. The world is not going to end if you lose this one, so live to fight another day.

SAY "THANK YOU"

- Thank supporters and sponsors of legislation you are interested in whether the legislation passes or fails.

- Write thank-you letters immediately after visits to your legislator.

- Write a letter of congratulation when your legislator is elected. If he is reelected, thank him for his past support on library issues. Volunteer to provide him with information about library services to youngsters. Money contributions to his campaign never hurt, nor does volunteering to work in his campaign.

- The legislature voted an increase in aid to school library media centers. Immediately write thank-you letters to your representatives.

- The governor mentioned library media centers in her State of the State address. Send a letter of thanks to let her know you appreciate her recognition of the importance of media centers to children's education.

INFLUENTIAL OTHERS

- While not elected officials, some people hold sway with those who are. Know who the "influentials" are and ask them to support libraries and to use their influence to get the library message to those who make decisions. If they won't, ask them how to go about doing it.

- People in the media (those who write for newspapers and magazines, those who report and comment on the news in the broadcast media, those who make decisions about what will be broadcast and printed) affect what news gets attention and what is ignored. Do your part in seeing that library issues get their fair share of the media pie, and that the information reported is accurate.

- Take the library message to the media. Librarians and advocates displayed signs outside NBC studios in New York City during National Library Week in 1995. After two days of seeing the librarians and their signs, the *Today* show hosts commented on the importance of libraries on their April 11 program. Two youngsters from North Salem, New York, School District, daughters of Rocco Staino, head librarian at the middle and high schools, held a National Library Week sign. Librarians Mary Shrodek, Barbara Paxson, and Diane Thomas of Warren, Ohio, Public Library, held a sign reading "Vote for Libraries" ("NLW on *Today*" 1995).

- Members of your state board of education (or whatever that body is called in your state) make educational policy including that dealing with libraries. Write letters to them, speak at their hearings, find out if libraries have a particular advocate in the group. If not, try to develop one. Provide them with information about kids and library services to youngsters.

Chapter 8

TELLING OTHERS WHAT YOU DO

REPORTS

Everybody hates to write reports. It seems such a waste of time: bringing all those numbers together, searching out the topics you worked on during the reporting period, putting it all down on paper. What a waste of time when you're pretty sure that nobody reads them. They just go into a file in the principal's office or, even worse, are dropped in the wastebasket. Some principals don't even want reports. They are concerned about the time you spend on them as well as the time they must spend on them—if they read them at all.

Reports, however, don't have to be all that bad. Even if your administrator doesn't ask for them, it's a good idea for you to prepare a simple report every month or two, just for your own benefit. Whatever time span you choose, stick to it so your statistics can be compared later. Reports provide data about our programs to decision makers, both in the building and the district. These numbers can be helpful to us in supporting our requests for materials, equipment, and staff and as we plan for the future, prepare our budgets, and evaluate our programs. Accountability is demonstrated through our documenting library media center activity.

Reports can also constitute an important part of public relations. We know that many people who should know better lack a basic understanding of what goes on in a library media center and how media center activities connect with children's education. They may have skewed or incomplete notions that need adjusting. Reports are a means to keep these people abreast of media center activities. A "Feedback Coupon" in the report gives your reader an easy way to respond with questions, comments, and requests for more information. Such a coupon lets all our readers know that we welcome hearing from them.

DIFFERENT REPORTS FOR DIFFERENT PEOPLE

Everyone in the community should be kept informed about the library media program, but tailor your report to your audience. What you say to teachers may be very different from what you want to emphasize to parents. Your report may be one sheet or several pages folded into a brochure. A report cannot and should not try to tell everything that went on in the media center. It may be a brief article or information reported in a box in the school district newspaper. For all, however, it is impossible to overemphasize the student-centered activities in the library media center. Everything we report should point to the way media center services are used by students. (Remember the "so-what factor" from chapter 2?) Our reports tell our readers about the broad range of media center activities and the direct application of these activities to students' educational progress, and to the kinds of employees, employers, parents, and voters they will become.

You want your report to be read, so make it eye-catching, different, and easy to read. Use headings, short sentences, and clear, simple writing. Your report should not be a tedious burden for either your reader or you as you prepare it (see Figure 8–1). Consider some of these suggestions for collecting data and for different report formats.

GATHER INFORMATION

- Cut old file folders into strips about three inches wide and keep one tucked under the edge of your desk blotter. Jot down during the day items that you may want to use in a report. Report information will come also from your class-schedule book and your circulation and attendance records. Keep all these items for your own use and also pull from them information for reports you send out.

- Take photos of students in the library media center and use them on the report cover or in the body of the report. Pictures of youngsters involved in library media activities add impact to your student-centered reports, and photographs photocopy surprisingly well.

REPORT FORMATS

- Once a year do a report in a "Book of Lists" format. Think up some headings (e.g., 5 Met Needs; 5 Unmet Needs; 10 Most Used Services and/or Materials; 8 Most Frequently Heard Complaints) and fill in under the heading (see Figure 8–2). Number the items on your list and make then short and

Figure 8–1 Did You Know?

DID YOU KNOW?

. . . that today (Tuesday, April 30) is School Library Media Day? We're not making it up; it's *official!* The governor has proclaimed School Library Media Day throughout the state to focus attention on the vital role school library media centers play in the educational process.

In light of this fact, it is necessary for us to abandon (temporarily) our customary modesty in order to (1) point out to our colleagues that there are indeed many worthwhile materials and services available in our-and-your-school library media center that you may be unaware of and (2) to encourage you to make use of some of them.

For example: Have you recently (or ever) used any of our

24,646	BOOKS? (+ paperbacks)
1,186	RECORDS AND TAPES?
2,216	SLIDES?
Many	PHOTOGRAPHS, MAPS, AND POSTERS?
478	ART REPRODUCTIONS?
2,105	MICROFICHE ITEMS? (newspapers and other goodies)
46 drawers	VERTICAL FILES?
473	VIDEOTAPES? (including motion pictures)
176	MAGAZINE SUBSCRIPTIONS?
6	COMPUTERS?
1	MIGHTY PHOTOCOPIER?
Numerous	DATABASES?

—AND Interlibrary Loan Services for what we don't have?

Our average daily attendance is 624 and our average daily circulation is 375*, so you can see that *someone* is making good use of our materials and services.

In addition to the usual library media services, we offer coffee, tea, the occasional cookie, as well as solicited and unsolicited opinions in the areas of financial planning, career counseling, affairs (foreign and domestic), health, getting along with the boss(es), and whether there is life on other planets. Please specify your area of need.

> For those who couldn't spare the time to read the preceding, we offer at this point a précis:
>
> Existing (as we do) only to serve you (as it were), we feel it would be mutually beneficial (job-wise) if you would make use of our facilities and suggest new materials and services to us so that we can continue to exist (as we do) only to serve you, etc. (only better). Get it? (at the library media place).

* and the rip-off rate is enormous!

Figure 8–2 Sample from List of Lists Report

**Report
November–December 19—
List of Lists**

5 MET NEEDS

1.   New photocopiers installed in Library and AV.
2.   Improved communication through more memos to faculty.
3.   New shelving arrived and set up.
4.   New half-time position added to library media staff.
5.   New roof effectively keeps out the rain, cause for *great* jubilation!

5 UNMET NEEDS

1.   Cleaning and maintenance less than satisfactory.
2.   Plans for shifting ninth grade to high school incomplete.
3.   Lack of districtwide coordination of library media program.
4.   Great gaping holes in the ceiling still unrepaired.
5.   Cable has not yet been restored. (Taken down by roofer.)

Figure 8–2 (cont.)

9 MOST USED SERVICES AND/OR MATERIALS

1. More than 12,000 students (an average of 369 per day) came to the LMC.
2. An average of 19 teachers per day used AV equipment.
3. Class groups (101) came in for library instruction and/or research.
4. Materials (49) were borrowed from other libraries or loaned to them.
5. An average of 139 magazines a day were checked out.
6. Library users took out some 294 books per day.
7. Prepared 26 bibliographies for teachers' classes.
8. Instructed students in the use of the microfilm reader/printer, the laminator, and computer on-line services.
9. Computers booked solid every period.

8 MOST FREQUENTLY HEARD COMPLAINTS

1. There are not enough video units.
2. Photocopiers are too slow.
3. It's too noisy in the library.
4. It's too quiet in the library.
5. There are not enough computer stations.
6. It's too warm in the library.
7. It's too cold in the library.
8. It's too dirty in the library (and somebody saw a mouse!).

snappy (too chilly in the library; too hot in the library). This kind of report gives you an opportunity to highlight some statistics, the classes you've worked with, and problems you need to address—plus you can work in a little humor, which is always important.

- Prepare a list of "Little Known Facts About the Library Media Center" to send to teachers and administrators. "Did you know that in October . . . ?" then list activities that took place; some attendance figures (12,126 student came to the media center—that's 12 visits per student!); the number of new materials added to the collection; some humor (168 cups of coffee were poured by the librarian, 13 were actually drunk); the number of teachers who used library media services (we know the 5 who did not come in—what can we do for you?).

- At the top of the page write: "So Far This Month, We Have:" then spell out the name of your media center down the left margin in capital letters, one letter under another (see Figure 8–3). Use each letter to begin a strong verb to start a phrase that describes an activity in the media center during the

Figure 8–3 So Far This Year Report

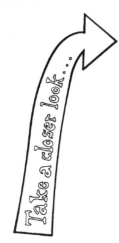

For Your Information

So Far This Year We Have:

Been ripped off twice (VCRs)
Extended library media services to the entire high-school staff
Encouraged more and more students to read for pleasure
Celebrated going on-line with the library media catalog
Hoped that the leaky roof would be repaired

Selected and added 811 new books to the collection
Offered teachers curriculum support in materials for health, social studies,
    English, art, science, mathematics, careers
Urged, with great success, a building-wide bibliographic form
Tagged 192 outworn and outdated books "Withdrawn"
Hosted the 3rd Annual Faculty Brown Bag Lunch

Had innumerable equipment breakdowns
Instructed 322 classes in library and information skills
Given service on the District Staff Development Committee
Helped Mrs. Ponzi with plans for an Ethnic Sharing program

Served as coordinators (with guidance) of the College Day Fair
Compiled 26 brand new book lists
Hesitated and counted to ten on several occasions
Ogled the faculty workroom at nearby Overton H.S.
Observed Black History Month and Women's History Month
Located information and loaned materials to other library media centers in the district

Loaned 50,000 plus items
Issued invitations that were accepted to department chairs to hold department meetings in the library
Believed that lost funding will be restored
Relieved several students by keeping our cool
Attended the state library media association conference
Rejoiced in the acquisition of a new photocopier that does wondrous things
Yelled and screamed at students for yelling and screaming in the library

Mounted 10 attention-attracting bulletin boards and displays
Erased the writing on library tables—again and again
Decided, after comparing war stories at the conference, that B.S.H.S. is the *best* school anywhere
Inaugurated a new system to get info to you faster
Appreciated cooperation of teachers and administrators

Continued active involvement in the School Library System
Entertained 106 parents at Open House Night
Noted the loyalty and hard work of our volunteers
Tried to be calm and cool in stressful situations
Enjoyed working with Mr. Thompson's EMR classes
Recognized that library media services *are* accepted as an integral part of the educational program
    at B.S.H.S.

B.S.H.S. Library Media Center

report period: Accommodated, Extended, Instructed, Inaugurated, Hosted, Deplored, Encouraged, etc. It is not difficult to work in statistics, activities, appreciation for support from administrators, addition of new materials, concern about things you want to change. Single-spacing, with double spaces at the end of individual words in the center's name, will yield about forty to forty-five lines on the page. Try to keep the length of each item to one line.

- A report that goes out to the community should be in language everyone understands, should contain many headings that guide the reader to different types of information, should emphasize students and how they benefit from library media services. Make the report eye-catching, clear, simple.

- Format an annual report to look like a tabloid newspaper. Write short paragraphs using your information, and design your headlines to grab attention like the ones you read at the supermarket checkout line.

ANNUAL REPORTS

- Once in a great while, give your administrators a nitty-gritty, "The State-of-the-Library Report." Pull out all the stops and include attendance, circulation, classes taught (on what topics), your professional activities outside the school, public relations activities, additions to the collection, comparisons with last year. While boring, this stuff is essential in supporting requests for increases in staffing, materials budget, and space. You may also discover areas from which funds can be shifted to a section of your budget where the need is greater.

- Base your annual report on goals you set at the beginning of the school year. Using each goal as a heading, throughout the year keep notes and statistics on related activities. If you did not achieve a goal completely, indicate what has been done and how you plan to work toward it next year. If you discovered that a goal was inappropriate and was abandoned along the way, explain why.

FLYERS, HANDOUTS, ETC.

Although there is a lot more to public relations than flyers and handouts, they are a means through which you can communicate with your publics, and someone has said that public relations equals communications. This means that you must be fiendishly clever with these paper pieces if you are to attract your readers' attention.

How many times have you stood in the front office and seen teachers at their mailboxes drop communications from you directly into the trash can without ever looking at them? It hurts, doesn't it? You are trying to communicate some important information (or perhaps not so important), and they don't even look at it. When confronted, teachers and others say they have too much junk mail to plow through, it is always deadly dull, and they either know all that stuff already or couldn't care less. Knowing why they don't read it gives you what you need to know to turn around the situation.

Make your messages to the faculty witty, brief, and interesting. Not every message is of life-and-death importance, so use a little humor. Occasionally send a message that is not at all important, just amusing, and maybe a little zany. Let them know you are still there. Your audiences will come to appreciate and look forward to the breezy flyers you send out (see an example in figure 8–4).

Figure 8–4 Gotta Do Flyer

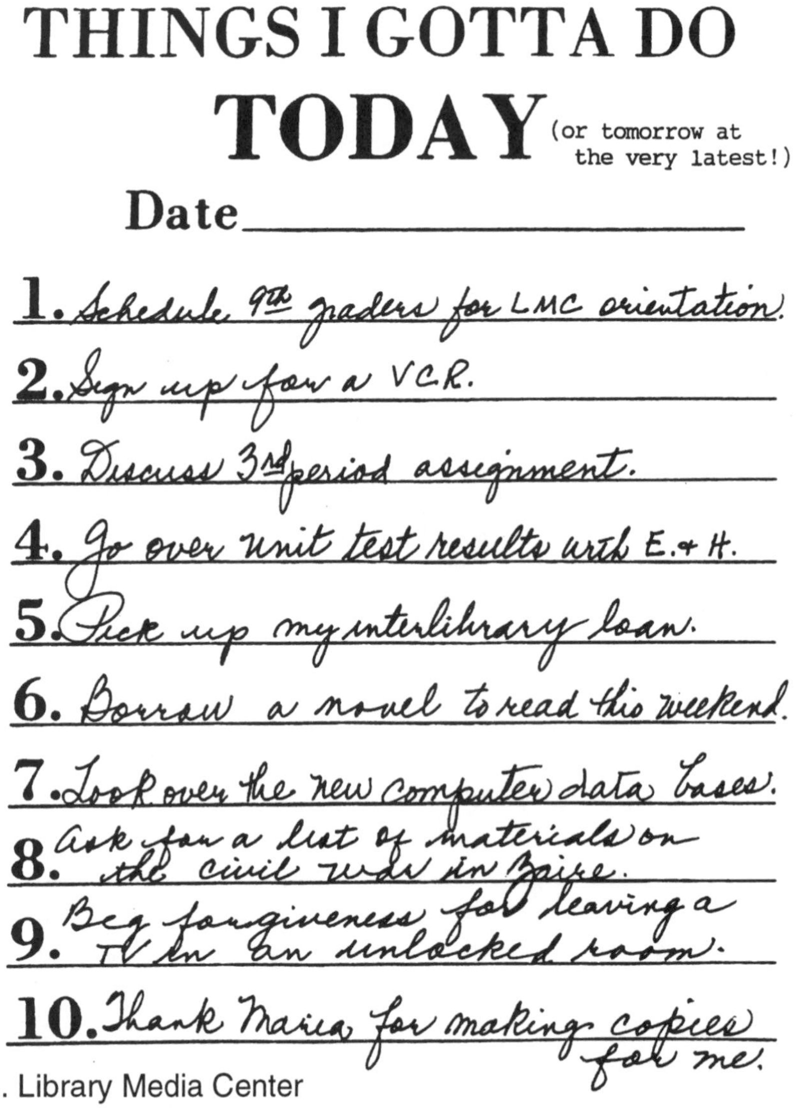

THINGS I GOTTA DO
TODAY (or tomorrow at the very latest!)

Date_____

1. Schedule 9th graders for LMC orientation.

2. Sign up for a VCR.

3. Discuss 3rd period assignment.

4. Go over unit test results with E. & H.

5. Pick up my interlibrary loan.

6. Borrow a novel to read this weekend.

7. Look over the new computer data bases.

8. Ask for a list of materials on the civil war in Zaire.

9. Beg forgiveness for leaving a TV in an unlocked room.

10. Thank Maria for making copies for me.

B.S.H.S. Library Media Center

Use colored papers for your billets-doux. Think of them as love letters in that you are wooing the recipients to become library media users and supporters! Once you have trained them to recognize that those bright green (or whatever) papers are from the media center, they won't be able to wait to read your message. You will discover that more and more of your printed messages are actually being read, that your message got through, that at least it was eyeballed before it was tossed into the wastebasket. Of course, you hope they are being filed in those folders you distributed at the beginning of the year!

Printed materials you send out to the community may express a more serious message and should be written more formally. If you send flyers by mail, get student or adult volunteers to address them by hand, and use postage stamps, not meter-printed postage. Research shows that these two practices almost guarantee that the envelope will be opened and the contents read (Dillman 1978). Computer-printed labels and printed postage are too closely associated with junk mail, which is frequently tossed aside without even being opened. Select the proper format as well as the proper style for your message according to the audience receiving it.

Build a collection of clip-art books and circulate a list of them to teachers. Once your printed materials begin receiving the recognition they so richly deserve, others will want to improve theirs and will come to you for suggestions and graphics. You will find that the clip-art books get a lot of use from students, teachers, and administrators. You will have raised the standard for flyers and printed materials in your building, and the library media center will have added yet another item to its list of available services.

GUARD AGAINST POMPOSITY

In your written communications, avoid the temptation to throw your weight around. Don't be like the building instructional equipment coordinator who wrote his end-of-semester request for the return of equipment as though he had more authority than the superintendent. He always used formal, white, school stationery for his letter, which was made up of several single-spaced paragraphs written in the finest educationese. There were always a few threats aimed at those who did not follow his detailed instructions for returning equipment. At the bottom were his full name and title, which grew more grandiose with each new letter. It was certainly not his intention to be humorous, but his letters generated a few hearty laughs—although not very many on-time equipment returns. So I repeat: Avoid pomposity. (See figures 8–5 and 8–6 for examples of how to carry this off.)

Flyers, handouts, and other printed materials can be effective ways to build a positive image for the library media center and increase understanding of and support for your library media program. Here are some suggestions for printed material you may want to produce, as well as some pointers that may make their production easier and more effective.

Figure 8–5 Letting Us In Flyer

To: The Faculty

From: The Library Media People

Re: Letting us in on your plans

Date: March 15, 19—

WHEREAS,   The library media center seats 80; and
            The number of students who appear each period is 50–60 or
            so; and

WHEREAS,   Some *well-trained* teachers SCHEDULE their classes into
            the library media center, which adds 20–30 more; and

WHEREAS,   Some OTHER teachers (note we've used no pejorative
            terminology*) send groups to the library media center (UN-
            ANNOUNCED) from their classes;

RESOLVED,   That in the future names of such teachers will be placed on a
            list and . . .

* It is not our function to condemn but to try to make you better persons.
Actually, we can serve your students better if we don't have to push our way
through the mob.

Figure 8–6 End of the Year Countdown

May 15, 19—

TO: The Faculty

FROM: The Library Media Group

RE: Library Media Center Countdown

The end of the marking period is only three weeks away (who'd believe it!), and we are beginning to be a tad anxious about getting back several thousand books, putting our shelves in order, and preparing for that annual, much looked-forward-to-festival (inventory) lovingly described by library insiders as THE PITS.

Consequently, all books and AV materials are due in the center on or before May 31. Students may work in the center and use materials here through June 7. The week of June 10–14 we will be engaged in inventory when no one in his/her right mind would want to be near us. Students doing make-up work of an emergency nature that requires library media materials may find work space here. Send them (they must possess great personal courage) with a note. We will take care of them. Sounds ominous, doesn't it?

If these plans create problems for you or your students, please contact us so we can make whatever special arrangements are needed. Deep down inside we strive to please.

YOUR TRADEMARKS

- Develop a logo as your media center's identifying mark. Enlist the aid of art students, an art teacher, a design class, or use the national library logo. Don't try to squeeze books, periodicals, computers, tapes, motion pictures, and videos into one small drawing; keep it simple. Then use your logo on everything that goes out from the media center.

- Buy the most brightly colored paper you can find to use for your flyers and make it part of your center's identity. Although more expensive than plain white paper or pastel, it is effective. People will come to know immediately that loud-colored pages mean they have another of those bright, sassy, witty, informative handouts from the library, something that will break dull routine and that they will enjoy reading. If you can't find the money in your budget or from funds you raised, you may have to take it from your own pocket. The results are worth it.
  Guard this paper with your life. Do not share it with the guidance department or anybody else who admires it and wants to use some. Refusing is not hard, especially if you paid for it yourself.

- Buy some rubber stamps and different colored ink pads to use on the notes you send out. One excellent source is Kidstamps, whose stamps are school and/or library oriented, have characters from children's literature, and encourage reading. Ask for a copy of their catalog (see List of Sources).

GATHER IDEAS

- Collect quotes that strike your fancy in a folder on your desk. Jot down some student comments or clip quotes from newspapers, magazines (not the library's, we hope) or photocopy them from a book you're reading. These can be about libraries, schools, kids, teachers. They should be short, witty, poignant, snappy, serious, irreverent, or none of the above. Now and then select several, arrange them with an attention-attracting graphic (see Figure 8–7), and print it on some of that bright paper you hold so precious. Faculty and administrators need a lift occasionally. Be sure the media center's name (and logo, if you have one) are on the paper.

- The polite word is "adapt." Actually you can "borrow" and "steal" ideas from many sources. You could probably do a terrific job without ever having an original idea, just going through life "adapting" other people's ideas to fit your situation. Warning: it almost never works, however, to take an idea from elsewhere and use it unchanged. Everyone's needs differ from everyone else's. Plus, be careful of copyright infringement. Read a few articles to make sure what you're doing is legal, and cite sources if required or attribute generously when not.

Figure 8–7 Quote for the Week

Quote for the week:

"Treat people as if they were what they ought
to be, and help them to become what
they are capable of being." —Goethe

Next week's quote (sent to you now to
conserve paper):
"The best thing to spend on
children is your time."

And, in closing:

"The secret to life is looking
good at a distance." —Snoopy

The above is brought to you by those friendly people at BSHS Library Media Center

- Watch for interesting lettering you can use on memos or note paper (see Figure 8–8). Photocopy, enlarge or reduce, clip, and mount on your master. Type in any other information or heading. Use other interesting fonts available on your computer programs.

- Public relations committees in state and national associations frequently offer Shop and Swap sessions at conferences. They ask you to send, prior to the conference, multiple copies of materials you have produced, and at the session you can pick up copies of materials that others have done. Even if you don't contribute your own materials, you can attend and take things others have produced. Wonderful ideas!

DESIGNING AND PRODUCING

- Although you will print your flyers on colored paper be sure to place your original on white paper. Print several copies on white and carefully save them in a folder marked "Originals" in your file. You will surely need to reprint more copies (perhaps to take to an idea-sharing meeting), and copies made from colored paper come out, at the very best, gray.

- Communication is a two-way street, so include a feedback coupon on appropriate publications so your readers can provide you with their reactions. Do all you can to make it easy for others to communicate with you.

- Keep your publications eye-catching, clear, and simple. Use language your readers will understand; avoid jargon.

- A photocopier that enlarges and reduces copy to fit the space available is a wonderful thing to have access to (see Figure 8–9 for a list of other useful tools). Note: the real justification for having an enlargement feature on your

Figure 8–8 Lettering for Note Paper

Figure 8–9 Tools for Making Flyers

Tools to have on hand to make flyers:

- Sharp pointed scissors. Nail scissors have good points and their curved blades make cutting curves a whiz.
- Straight-edge scissors
- Correction fluid
- Double-sided tape or rubber cement
- A straight-edge (to draw the line we sometimes say we can't draw).
- A paper cutter
- A photocopier

---

copier is so materials can be reproduced in a print size large enough to be useful for visually impaired students. This is essential for copies of tests, pages from books, articles from magazines for those students. If you do not already have such a machine in your building, ask some teachers to join you in a campaign to get one. Teachers will love you for this.

- Always make and save extra copies of the publications you produce. Keep them neatly in the folders so you can easily retrieve them. Students come in asking for materials handed out the day they missed class, teachers want copies of a bibliography you did last year, you want copies to take to an idea-sharing meeting with other librarians. (Of course, if you don't have copies left you can print more using the white originals you had the foresight to save.)

- Design attractive cover sheets for the lists you distribute to teachers and others (see Figure 8–10).

- Use the names of students, teachers, community visitors, and others when appropriate in your printed materials. Parents love to see their children mentioned, and everyone wants his name in print.

- Use an instant-picture camera to photograph students engaged in media center activities. These reproduce quite well on the photocopier and enhance the appearance of reports, brochures, and other materials.

LEARN AND TEACH

- Plan to attend a PR workshop at your state or national association conference. You benefit in terms of how-to-do-it, and you pick up ideas that you can adapt for your own use.

Figure 8–10 Magazine List Cover

In the library, check the *Library Magazine List* for information on our collection of noncurrent periodicals.

If you would like to use a periodical we do not have, perhaps we can borrow it for you from another library. Please speak to Helen Flowers about it.

BEECH SOUTH HIGH SCHOOL
LIBRARY MEDIA CENTER

October 19—

- Offer to present a workshop on flyers, handouts, and other printed materials at your district library media council meetings, your regional school library system workshop, or your professional association's state conference. Teachers in your building and district may also be interested in such a presentation. Discuss it with your in-service coordinator.

GRAPHICS AND CLIP ART

- A good source of inexpensive publications that feature copyright-free illustrations is Dover Publications. Write for their free catalog (see List of Sources).

- ALA Graphics publishes *Quick Clip Art* in both print and disk formats. You will find this listed in the *ALA Graphics* catalog, which is available free from ALA (see List of Sources).

- Keep a clip-art file. This sounds all formal and well organized, and it would be lovely to have folders of pictures of kids at computers, of seasonal pictures, of faces of great people, etc. In real life, however, there doesn't seem to be time to do all that sorting and arranging, and some things just don't fit into one category. Consequently, they are more likely just to pile up in a copier-paper box lid. But you can probably live with that.

- Graphics—the pictures you use on your publications—should be pictures that will reproduce well on photocopies, and this usually means line drawings without a lot of shading and half-tones. Soon after beginning your collection, you'll find you won't be able to read a newspaper, a magazine, or a throwaway advertisement without seeing something you can adapt for your use. Tear it out or photocopy it and drop it in your box.

- Use humorous drawings and sayings on the bibliographies and study sheets you prepare to use with classes. Your brightly colored pages will be easy for students to locate in their notebooks. Ask a student volunteer to three-hole punch them so they are less likely to be lost.

- Look into the availability of computer programs for clip art and for producing covers, flyers, and other handouts. Print a master copy on white paper and use that for photocopiers.

SOME PRACTICAL FORMS

Create for yourself and other members of the media center staff (whose responsibilities call for it) some interesting note paper for communicating with faculty, administrators, students. Stay away from tired old "From the Desk of . . . " that everybody else uses. You may want several different styles to fit your mood and/or your message (see the sample in Figure 8–11). One style does not fit all occasions. (We are not talking here about formal stationery for formal communications.) Use your colored paper, of course.

Figure 8–11 Express Mail Note Paper

It is also a good idea to make up forms to use for routine communications (see figures 8–12 and 8–13). Make them as professional looking as you can. Use your colored paper and the snappiest graphics you have.

Figure 8–12 A Routine Communication Form

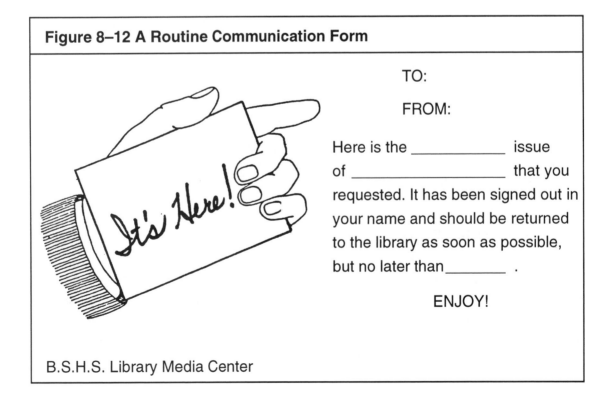

Figure 8–13 All-Purpose-Fill-In-the-Blanks Letter

LIBRARY MEDIA ALL-PURPOSE-FILL-IN-THE-BLANKS LETTER

Date _____

TO: _____
 ___ Whom it may concern
 ___ The kids in your class
 ___ Everybody out there

FROM:
 ___ Helen Flowers   ___ Eileen Mayott
 ___ Eileen Mulcahy   ___ Maria Sparacio
 ___ Pat Veraldo   ___ All of these
 ___ Vicki Mahr   ___ None of these
 ___ Connie De Louise   ___ Guess who
 ___ Georgette Brosnan   ___

RE:
 ___ Books   ___ Software
 ___ Tapes   ___ Computers
 ___ Overdues   ___ Reserve materials
 ___ Magazines   ___ Videotaping
 ___ Videos   ___ Personal message
 ___ Money   ___ Your cooperation
 ___ BIG trouble   ___ Beginning of school
 ___ End of school   ___ Guess what

MESSAGE:

 PLEASE:
 ___ Pick up materials we're holding.   ___ Come see what we have for you.
 ___ Come for coffee, tea, or soup.   ___ Help prevent rioting and pillaging.
 ___ Call your wife/husband/other.   ___ Suggest titles to purchase.
 ___ Inform me of your plans.   ___ Return your equipment.
 ___ Preview materials.   ___ Come see new materials.
 ___ Your copies are ready.   ___ We finished your project.
 ___ Schedule your classes.   ___ Enjoy yourself.
 ___ Return things, finished or not.   ___ Stop suggesting titles to purchase for your class.

THANKS FOR:
 ___ Previewing materials.   ___ Sending in your classes.
 ___ Getting your equipment back.   ___ All those books!
 ___ Your donation(s).   ___ Your prompt reply.
 ___ Helping out.   ___ Just being our friend.
 ___ Your anticipated cooperation.   ___ Nothing.

AND:
 ___ Haven't seen you lately, what are you up to?
 ___ We know what you're up to!
 ___ You've been forgiven.
 ___ That's fine with me.
 ___ I refuse to believe the dog ate the whole thing.
 ___ We've got to stop meeting like this.
 ___ We've got to start meeting more often.
 ___ It couldn't happen to a nicer person.

Chapter 9

SPEAK OUT FOR LIBRARIES: SPEECHES AND INTERVIEWS

HOW TO GAIN CONFIDENCE AND BE AN EFFECTIVE SPEAKER

Ask yourself, "What is the most frightening situation in which I could find myself?" If you are like about 70 percent of the population, your answer will be, "Standing before an audience to make a speech." Even among those who do not name making a speech as their greatest fear, a large number of people include it as one of their top five.

What is it we fear about speaking before an audience?

- I don't know enough to make a speech.
- I don't know what to say.
- I will bore the audience.
- I will forget my speech.
- I won't be able to control my voice.
- I will come off looking like a fool before these people.

All these reasons can be categorized as "lacking self-confidence." When you are invited to give a short speech (we're not talking about a State-of-the-Union Address) supporting libraries, your immediate reaction may be one of horror. "Not me! I could never speak before a group."

GAINING SELF-CONFIDENCE

One way to begin working to overcome stage fright and developing self-confidence is to gather your information and then to imagine yourself successfully doing the thing you fear. Sit down in a comfortable chair in a quiet place, put your head back and your feet up, and in this relaxed, comfortable position, picture yourself in a professional-looking outfit having a good hair day. See yourself on a platform or at a head table listening to someone introduce you. You hear applause and see yourself, with every indication of confidence, step up to speak.

A hush falls, and the audience waits expectantly for you to begin. Your words about libraries and their importance in schools and in the community flow effortlessly, and the audience hangs on every one. You are articulate, passionate, and persuasive. You make your points, offer examples, and tell the audience specifically what you want them to do and how their actions will benefit themselves and their community.

When you finish speaking, you feel the warmth of applause wash over you and hear words of appreciation from individuals. It is magic! You have held the audience in the palm of your hand. This is an experience you want to have in fact, not just in your imagination.

In *The King and I*, Anna tells her young son how she overcomes fear. She advises him to stand straight and whistle a happy tune whenever he is frightened so no one will know that he is afraid. You may not want to whistle a tune, happy or otherwise, as you approach the speaker's stand, but you may "think" one. Anna's advice is good, because when you act confidently, you gain confidence.

Your dream does not show you preparing your speech. In the real world, however, you must gather information and organize and prepare it carefully. If you are not fully prepared, no amount of showmanship will save you.

PREPARING YOUR SPEECH

Learn who your audience will be, find out how large a group to expect, and what the group's interests are. Are you speaking to a group of parents concerned about their children's education, to a group of people dedicated to cutting taxes, or to a group of business people concerned about the economic situation in their community? Tailor your speech to the concerns of the audience.

Don't be like the befuddled horseman in Stephen Leacock's story, "Gertrude the Governess," who leaped to his horse and "rode off in all directions." Organization and preparation are essential to being an effective speaker.

- Write out your speech so you are sure to cover all the points you want to make. Don't try to memorize it, but do internalize the ideas and concepts you will cover and the order in which you will use them.

- Do not read your speech. Have as notes a word or two that will bring to your mind each point you want to make. Use cards, which are easy to handle. Sheets or slips of paper flutter and make rustling noises and are difficult to control. Print the words on your cards in large, very black letters that you will easily see when occasionally glancing at them.

- Rehearse your speech with a friend and tape or videotape it to hear how it sounds. Do you modulate your voice? Are your points arranged in a logical manner? Does it make sense? You want to talk to your audience as though you are having a conversation with a friend. Videotaping is especially helpful because not only can you hear your voice, but also you can see how you look. Do you appear relaxed? Do you smile? Are your gestures natural looking? Library services and their support is a topic about which you are passionate. Be sincere, let your audience know that you mean what you are saying and that you are eager to share your concerns about libraries with every member of your audience.

- Have a clear, concrete message. Use stories about real people to whom you assign names (maybe not real ones). Use details and dialogue, and speak with expression, using body language. Speak in language the audience will understand, avoiding jargon and acronyms.

- Establish a link for your audience that demonstrates why what you are saying is important to them and to their community. Tell them exactly what you want them to do and how their actions will benefit them.

- Identify yourself with the audience. Use the pronoun "you" rather than "they," or "we" instead of "you."

- Make your audience a partner in your talk. Ask for a response to a question or a show of hands. Call on them to do something.

- Know how much time you are allotted on the program and do not go past it. Leave them wanting more.

- If you have handouts, be sure you have more than enough. Distribute them at the end of your talk. While you are speaking, you want the attention of the audience on you, not on your handouts.

- Invite questions from the audience. During the preparation of your talk think of questions you may be asked and prepare answers. Ask the friend you rehearsed with to pose some really hostile questions. Be prepared for those listeners who do not share your point of view. Do not reply to these questions in a hostile manner. Stay calm. Preparing in advance for troublesome questions can increase your confidence. Remember, you are in charge.

MAKING THE SPEECH

- Arrive at the meeting place before the program begins. Move through the room speaking with people and shaking hands. When you get up to speak, people will feel they know you, feel friendly toward you, and want you to do well.

- When you are introduced, move briskly to the speaker's stand. Take a deep breath and stand tall. Look directly into the eyes of the audience and begin to talk confidently. Move around as you speak. It proves that you are alive and have not become permanently attached to the speaker's stand. It forces the audience to watch you and to see where you move to next, and helps hold the attention of the audience. Moving about also helps reduce your own stress.

- Keep in mind that you have earned the right to speak about libraries. You know from experience what libraries mean in the lives of people. You feel deeply about libraries and literacy, and when your listeners see your eagerness and hear the enthusiasm in your voice, they will pay attention and connect to your message.

- Do not be overly concerned about stage fright. It comes from physical changes in your body as it prepares itself to deal with a challenge. Your pulse beats faster and your respiration speeds up. These changes make you more alert and help you speak more fluently and with greater intensity. In all likelihood, the audience will not physically attack you.

- You have an interesting topic about which you could speak for days. Chances are, however, that twenty minutes is all the time you will have. You will be amazed, however, at how fast the time goes, so arrange in advance with someone in the audience to let you know as you approach the end of your time. Don't forget to look at that person occasionally.

- Your audience will be fascinated by your examples, your enthusiasm, and your convictions. No one will be bored. As you speak directly to individuals your fears will melt away, your words will flow in a strong voice, and you will feel poised and filled with self-confidence.

- Thank the group for the opportunity to speak to them, then go search out other opportunities. Let it be known that you are available to speak about libraries and the important role they can play in people's lives, in the education of children, in lifelong learning, in the economic well-being of the community. The more you speak, the better speaker you will become. Don't delay. Speak out for libraries!

SO, YOU'RE GOING TO BE INTERVIEWED ON TELEVISION?

Your regional library organization has arranged a breakfast meeting for librarians and local legislators to thank them for their past support and to discuss the need for increased funding for library services. In preparation for the meeting, you called the TV station and invited them to send a reporter. Because a gathering of legislators is often a newsworthy event, the station decides to cover the meeting, and asks you as an organizer of the function to participate in a short interview that will be conducted on the day of the meeting. You're going to be on the ten o'clock news!

Before the day arrives, watch the news programs with a new eye. Observe that the stories they report rarely last more than a minute or two, and the person being interviewed is onscreen for only ten to fifteen seconds. This tells you that there will be very little time to get your message across.

YOU, THE INTERVIEWEE

- Notice how public officials and other experienced interviewees respond to questions. They do not often directly answer the interviewer's questions, but use them as a bridge to get to the points they want to make. You should prepare two or three points you want to communicate about library services and, using the bridging technique, get your message across. Practice this with a friend asking you questions.

- Don't let the reporter make your statement for you—"Wouldn't you say . . . "—followed by a statement she wants you to agree with. Make your own statement, "Cynthia, more people use libraries. . . . "

- Avoid repeating negatives. If the reporter asks a hostile question, respond with a positive statement about libraries and librarians. "Why do librarians buy dirty books for children to read?" may be answered with "The librarian's job is to select quality books for children, and we are experts at doing that. We are eager to help parents choose appropriate books for their youngsters to read."

- Prepare some short, pithy statements—sound bites—to use. The reporter will include in the story only a small portion of what is said in the interview, so provide her with some quotable copy.

  — "Kids who aren't logged on and literate will be lost in the 21st Century."

  — "To invest in libraries is to invest in the future of our children and our nation."

  — "Librarians know how to get kids hooked on books. They'll be able to help you and your child."

— "Research shows that the highest achieving students come from schools with good library media centers."

— "Americans spend six times as much on home video games ($5.5 billion) annually as they do on school library materials for their children" (ALA 1995).

• As you find or think of other concise statements that make quick, clear points, jot them down and drop them into your file so you will be ready at a moment's notice.

And remember:

• Never respond to a question with "no comment."

• Nothing is ever "off the record."

• Your microphone is always on.

• Never assume you're off camera.

• Use simple language, no jargon or acronyms.

• Don't get angry.

• Keep your eyes on the interviewer (or on the camera, if you're speaking directly to the audience).

• Never watch the monitor.

HOW DO I LOOK?

For your moment in the spotlight, strive for a professional look by wearing a solid-color suit. (Suits are power dressing, and solid colors have a slimming effect; besides, bold plaids can be distracting.) Women should avoid jewelry such as charm bracelets that make noise that can be picked up by the microphone. Heavier than usual make-up will compensate for the bright TV lights that tend to make you look pale and washed out. Men may not like putting on make-up, but they, too, can appear washed out without it.

Adjust your clothing before the session begins. Straighten your skirt and jacket, adjust your collar, tie, or scarf. Don't play with your tie tack, your beads, the microphone, or your hair during the interview.

Relax. Be comfortable, not stiff. Hold your head up. Look interested. You're on television!

AFTERWORD

This book has given you some ideas that you can adapt to your own situation, but it cannot begin to tell you everything you need to know, and will know, after you have experienced practicing public relations regularly yourself. Public relations is people relations, and once it has become second nature to you, you will do it better and better and enjoy it more and more. You will instinctively gear yourself to each of your many publics. People do the very best kind of public relating when they love their work and enthusiastically talk about it. School library media specialists with a vision of all they can do to help kids become all they can be are naturals to become public relations experts.

REFERENCES

American Library Association. *Gotta Have a Gimmick*. Chicago: AASL Public Awareness Committee, 1993.

————. *Library Advocacy Now! Presenter's Guide*. Chicago: American Library Association, 1995.

Butler, David. "Toot Your Own Trumpet!" *The Book Report* 9(3) (November-December 1990): 22.

Dierksen, C. N., and Terry Oberg. "Students Are the Best Source of School Information for Parents." *Journal of Educational Communications* 5(1) (July 1981): 36–37.

Dillman, Don A. *Mail and Telephone Surveys: The Total Design Method*. New York: Wiley, 1978.

Hartzell, Gary N. *Building Influence for the School Librarian*. Worthington, OH: Linworth, 1994.

Lance, Keith Curry, Lynda Welborn, and Christine Hamilton-Pennell. *The Impact of School Library Media Centers on Academic Achievement*. Denver: Colorado Department of Education, 1992.

"NLW on *Today*." *American Libraries* 26(7) (July/August 1995): 627.

Saretsky, Cecile L. "Libraries After High School: Maintaining the Library Connection." *The Bookmark* 50(1) (Fall 1991): 72–74.

U.S. Department of Education, Office of Educational Research and Improvement. "Parents and Schools: Partners in Student Learning." *National Center for Educational Statistics*, October 1996, p. 7.

Werner, Emmy, and Ruth S. Smith. *Overcoming the Odds: High Risk Children from Birth to Adulthood*. Ithaca, NY: Cornell University Press, 1992.

SOME SOURCES OF POSTERS, CLIP ART, AND OTHER PROMOTIONAL MATERIALS

Write for catalogs.

ALA Graphics
American Library Association
50 East Huron Street
Chicago, Illinois 60611

Children's Book Council
568 Broadway
New York, New York 10012

Demco
Box 7488
Madison, Wisconsin 53707-7488

Dover Publications
31 East 2nd Street
Mineola, New York 11501

Highsmith Company, Inc.
W 5527 Highway 106
Box 800
Fort Atkinson, Wisconsin 53538-0800

JanWay Company
11 Academy Road
Cogan Station, Pennsylvania 17728-9300

Kidstamps
P.O. Box 18699
Cleveland Heights, Ohio 44118

Library of Congress
Center for the Book
Washington, DC 20540

Upstart Library Promotions
32 East Avenue
Box 889
Hagerstown, Maryland 21740

Wonderstorms
World Almanac Education
1278 West Ninth Street
Cleveland, Ohio 44113-1067

FOR FURTHER READING

American Library Association and the Association for Educational Communications and Technology. *Information Power: Guidelines for School Library Media Programs.* Chicago: American Library Association, 1988.

Bellman, Geoffrey M. *Getting Things Done When You Are Not in Charge.* San Francisco: Berrett-Koehler, 1992.

Bennis, Warren. *On Becoming a Leader.* Reading, MA: Addison-Wesley, 1989.

Chase's Annual Events: The Day-by-Day Directory. Chicago: Contemporary Books, annual.

Ekhaml, Leticia. "The Persuasive Power of Reciprocation." *School Library Media Activities Monthly* 11(9) (May 1995): 32–34.

Everhart, Nancy. "Library Aides: If You Fulfill Their Needs, They Will Come (and Work!)." *The Book Report* 13(1) (May–June 1994): 12–13.

Farmer, Lesley S. J. "Reap What You Sow: PR Benefits of Advising Students." *The Book Report* 13(1) (May–June 1994): 13–14.

Flowers, Helen F. "68 Ways to Catch a Teacher." *The Book Report* 4(2) (September–October 1985): 17, 20.

Great Library Promotion Ideas VI: JCD Library Public Relations Award Winners and Notables, 1990. Chicago: ALA, 1991.

Haycock, Ken. *Program Advocacy: Power, Publicity, and the Teacher-Librarian.* Englewood, CO: Libraries Unlimited, 1990.

Kollasch, Matthew. "D 'n' A" [Discipline and Access]. *Wilson Library Bulletin* 65(5) (January 1991): 67–71.

Krashen, Stephen. *The Power of Reading: Insights from the Research.* Englewood, CO: Libraries Unlimited, 1993. 33–41.

Liebold, Louise Condak. *Fireworks, Brass Bands, and Elephants: Promotional Events with Flair for Libraries and Other Nonprofit Organizations.* Phoenix: Oryx, 1986.

"Making the Most of the School Library." *The Book Report* 7(1) (May–June 1988): 10–21.

"Nine-Year-Old Praises Libraries in Chat with President Clinton." *American Libraries* 25(6) (June 1994): 478–79.

"Public Relations for the School Library." *The Book Report* 10(1) (May–June 1991): 14–27.

"Reaching Out to Parents and Community." *The Book Report* 14(1) (May–June 1995): 13–28.

Reardon, Kathleen Kelly. *They Don't Get It, Do They? Communication in the Workplace.* Boston: Little, Brown, 1995.

Shantz, Doreen. "Program Advocacy." *Emergency Librarian* 21(3) (January–February 1994): 22–25.

Sherman, Steve. *ABC's of Library Promotion.* 3d ed. Metuchen, NJ: Scarecrow, 1992.

Silva, Betty. "Advocacy—Whose Responsibility?" *CMLEA Journal* 16(1) (Fall 1992): 11–14.

Smallwood, Carol. "School Librarian a.k.a. Published Writer." *The Book Report* 13(3) (November–December 1994): 13–14.

Thibodeaux, Annette. "Promotional Materials." *The Book Report* 14(1) (May–June 1995): 19–20.

Tuggle, Ann Montgomery, and Dawn Hansen Heller. *Grand Schemes and Nitty-Gritty Details: Library PR That Works.* Littleton, CO: Libraries Unlimited, 1987.

INDEX

ABOUT THE AUTHOR

Helen Flowers served as a school library media specialist for 30 years, 28 of them in a high school on Long Island, New York. She holds a B.A. from Peabody College of Vanderbilt University; an M.S. from the School of Library Service, Columbia University; and an Ed.D. in Educational Administration from Hofstra University.

As an adjunct professor, she has taught Educational Public Relations at Hofstra, and library courses at both the Palmer School of Library and Information Science of Long Island University, and at the State University of New York at Stony Brook.

She is past-president of the New York Library Association (NYLA), as well as of the School Library Media Section of NYLA.

She served on her school district's Public Information Advisory Committee, and on the New York State Regents Advisory Council on Libraries, and was a delegate from New York to the White House Conference on Library and Information Services in 1991.

In retirement she and her husband make their home in North Carolina, where she continues to be a library advocate. She also sings in a women's chorus and in a small group called the Krazy Ladies' Vocal Ensemble and Rhythm Band.

2712